MW01204665

Psalms are for Praying
Toward a Mindset of Faith

By Rudolf E. Klimes, Ph.D.

Director, Bible Dialog Institute

LearnWell Press, Folsom, CA

Psalms are for Praying: Explore a Mindset of Faith

Copyright © 2009 Rudolf E. Klimes, Ph.D., D.Min.

Published by CreateSpace
for LearnWell Press, PO Box 1178, Folsom, CA 95763.

Edited by Anna Klimes, Ed.D.

Library of Congress Publication Data

Klimes, Rudolf E.

Psalms are for Praying: Explore a Mindset of Faith

ISBN 9781441405388

1. Bible Study-Psalms
2. Prayer
3. Bible Commentary- Psalms

www.learnwell.org

www.BibleD.org

edu@learnwell.org 916-984-7437

Contents

Dedicated to my grandchildren:

Justin Michael Borrowdale

Torin James Borrowdale

Tyler John Dougan

Hudson Emanuel Dougan

Part I: How to Pray the Psalms

"The Psalms have a unique place in the Bible because most of the Scripture speaks *to* us, while the Psalms speak *for* us...In the *Psalter* you learn about yourself. You find depicted in it all the movements of your soul, all its changes, its ups and downs, its failures and recoveries." *Athanasius of Alexandria*

"Every man, on every occasion, can find in the Psalms that which fits his needs..." *Martin Luther*

"Not the poverty of our own heart, but the riches of the Word of God must decide how we are to pray." *Dietrich Bonhoeffer in The Psalms - Prayer Book of the Bible*

Prayer is directly addressed to God, in which one enters God's domain. It is through talking to God that one accepts God's reality and sovereignty and one's own place in creation. *Rabbinical Tradition*

"By praying the Psalms back to God, we learn to pray in tune with the Father, Son, and Holy Spirit." *Ben Patterson*

1. A Mindset of Faith

Many of us start with a mindset of self. In most things we do, our self is the most important. We may rationalize and say that we are doing it all for others, but really we are most concerned that we look good and have more power than the next fellow. Self rules. Self is on the throne of the heart and influences all we do.

Self has a place in life. We need to know who we are, who we work for, and who we want to be. Self is the package that identifies us. We need it to make life goals, to evaluate our actions, and to measure how far we have come. We need it to serve others effectively. It is our starting point in life.

But a mindset of self is not enough. It limits us to centering our lives on ourselves. We easily become so absorbed in ourselves that we cannot serve others sincerely and worship God meaningfully.

We need a mindset of faith. We need to get outside of ourselves and trust our God and the trustworthy around us. That takes faith. That takes a larger power outside of ourselves to strengthen us for an adventurous journey. Often we have no idea where it will lead us. But if we trust the One who is good He will lead us in good paths.

The Psalms are prayers for that pilgrimage. They were written, sung and prayed from a mindset of faith for people who desire to develop a mind toward God. They are all about faith in a self-centered world. Psalms are for praying to get beyond self into the realm of faith.

God's hand is not so short that it cannot help. Isaiah 59:1. It is long enough. It can reach into the furthest corner. It can reach us and make us effective helpers. It can strengthen all we touch. In the Psalms, God reaches out to us. He gives us a mindset of faith.

2. How to Pray the Psalms Devotionally

Prayer is talking with God. We listen to God speaking through our experience, through nature, or through the Psalms and we respond with thoughts and/or words. God then in turn affirms our feeble attempts to communicate with Him and assures us through the Bible of His love and help. Our mind is set on faith.

When praying the Psalms, we minimize our common physical environment and focus on God's presence and His Glory. In our hearts, we enter the Kingdom of God and get immersed in His Wisdom.

We move from our physical surroundings toward faith. Generally we are set in a pattern dominated by our senses and our own thinking. In the life of faith we leave the ordinary behind and focus on the things of God. The Psalms are doors toward this life in God. As we read them prayerfully, we forget our troubles and take on God's concerns for our spiritual life.

The best prayers are the private ones when one is alone. Then there is no temptation for self-glorification. Not that the small-group prayers and public prayers before larger audiences are not valuable.

Read and pray the Psalms from the heart. Pray them as avenues of joy and roads to repentance. Memorize or meditate on them.

The Psalms are prayers for Jews (called Tehilim) and Christians alike. Moslems who worship one God, may also be helped by them. In addition, Hindus, Buddhists and people of other religions also use prayer and may find this volume relevant.

In the New Testament, we read: "Be filled with the Spirit by reciting psalms, hymns, and spiritual songs for your own good. Sing and make music to the Lord with your hearts." Ephesians 5:18-19

We may pray the verses of the Psalms in many different ways::

- a. Personalization, that is substituting "I" or "we" for names.
- b. Paraphrasing, that is putting the verse in your own words.
- c. Enlarging and expanding concepts.
- d. Selecting and marking a key word or key words.
- e. Asking questions and answering them.
- f. Experiencing and applying the concepts in the verses.
- g. Relating past experiences associated with the verses.
- h. Looking for ways to praise God.

"For every man, on every occasion, can find in the Psalms that which fits his needs, which he feels to be appropriate as if they had been set there just for his sake..." Martin Luther

C.S. Lewis found in the Psalms the same delight in God that made David dance. While it is also many other things, the psalms is a book of joy. Praise God joyfully.

One type of devotional prayers of the Psalms follows the pattern called "give, give and forgive." In the first section, "we give" God thanks for His blessings and we praise His name. Like in the Lord's Prayer, we address God as our Father.

In the second section, we ask God to "give us" our requests. In the Lord's Prayer we ask for God to give us our daily bread and deliver us from evil. We usually pray for wisdom to follow God and to respond to the service opportunities that He wants to place before us. The prayer is for us in the plural, since most prayers are community efforts that include all those with whom we associate. Most people think of this part as prayer and here they include all their needs and burdens.

The third section of this ppattern is for God to "forgive us" our blunders and sins. As we look to God, we realize our limitations and need for cleansing. We also forgive those who hurt us. We are forgiven in proportion to the degree to which we forgive others. We usually pray all this in the Name of Jesus, for He is the one who makes prayer effective.

Prayer may be spoken or thought sentences, cries from the innermost being or from the mouth, from the heart or from memory. God hears.

In summary, we pray to worship God, to seek His guidance, to ask for help, to confess our wrongs, or just to talk to a higher being.

There are some psalms in the Bible that are not part of the Book of Psalms. They include:

    a.   The Song of Moses, Exodus 15:1-18.
    b.   Hannah's Song, 1st Samuel 2:1-10.
    c.   Hezekiah's Recovery, Isaiah 38:10-20.
    d.   Jonah's Song, Jonah 2:2-9.
    e.   Mary's Magnificat, Luke 1:46-55.

Then there is the Lord's Prayer in Matthew 6: 9-13, which strictly speaking is not a psalm, but a prayer set later to music.

3. How to Pray the Psalms Searchingly

Some of us have many questions for God. We search for the answers God has for us. Thus we not only need to praise God, but we also explore who He is, what He does, and how He leads. That brings us to a prayer-centered, deeper searching of the Psalms.

Reading the Psalms and praying them is the devotional method of prayer. Praying them, analyzing them and seeking to apply each part of the Psalms is the searching method of prayer. This guide is a help for both methods. Here are some of the main searching approaches:

  a. Outlining paragraphs, and exploring patterns, themes, topics, summaries, or concepts.
  b. Studying the context to see what circumstances brought it about. You may use "who, what, when, where, why, how?"
  c. Analyzing key words by finding the central thoughts and related texts, commentary explanations, and other translations.
  d. Making personal applications of cases in an action-setting, such as short-and-long term projects, and portfolios.

Other searching approaches of Bible study and prayer may include

  a. Comparing two similar Psalms,
  b. Differentiating between the different parts of the Psalm,
  c. Writing a scope and sequence of events,
  d. Drawing a timeline of events,
  e. Showing what is open, hidden, blind, unknown.

4. The Psalms

The Psalms, the longest book of the Bible, are treasures of great spiritual insight. They are the response of David and other writers to the unfailing love of God. Most of the Bible deals with God speaking to men. The Psalms are men speaking to God. They are spiritual food for all that seek God.

The Psalms are an inspired collection of prayers, poems, meditations and songs in which people respond to God's love. Words or thoughts addressed to God are prayers. In the Psalms, we find not only deep expressions of pain and suffering, but also of faith and hope. The psalmists take all their concerns to their God, the good and the difficult, their joys and their sorrows.

All Psalms were set to music. They form the first song-book of the Hebrews. Singing them aided in their memorization. At one time, many or most Israelites had the Psalms memorized. Thus the Psalms formed the basis of their personal and group worship. All could always have an uplifting song in their hearts.

By praying the Psalms, we strengthen our relationship with God in at least two ways. The Psalms are Scripture, and reading the scripture holds a blessing by itself. By praying, we leave our local circumstances behind and enter the spiritual Kingdom of God. The path to God is by means of the Scriptures and by prayer.

Among early Christians, the Psalter also formed a song book and prayer book. Even though they were originally written to be accompanied by harps or other stringed instruments, for a long time, they were chanted without instruments. Starting in the 6th century, the Gregorian chants were sung by choirs. Later in the 15 century, the Genevan Psalter was one of the early song books of the Psalms.

The Psalms were written over a period of a thousand years from Moses to Ezra, from about 1400-400 BC. That is also when most of the Old Testament was written. Of the 150 psalms, 73 are attributed to David. Some 30 fragments of the Psalms were found among the Dead Sea Scrolls.

The Psalms may also be grouped according to the history of Israel around David's Covenant:

 a. INTRODUCTION: The Righteous Psalm 1—2.
 b. BOOK I: David and Saul, 3—41.
 c. BOOK II: David as King, 42-72.
 d. BOOK III: The Assyrian Crisis, 73—89.
 e. BOOK IV: The Temple and the Return of the Exile, 90-106.
 f. BOOK V: Praise on the Return, 107—145.
 g. CONCLUSION: Praise God, 146—150.

Many Christian scholars wrote that, if they could only have one book from the Bible, would choose the Psalms as that book. It is so full of experience, of worship, of spiritual wisdom.

Some of the Psalms are historical, others Messianic (dealing with Christ), prophetic, experiential or penitential. Some of the Psalms that called down curses on the enemies of God were appropriate at that time but must be carefully used today.

There is a close association between the experiences of the psalmist, Israel and the Lord Jesus Christ.

Jesus knew the Psalms and quoted, among others, from Psalm 8, 16, 22, 23, 31, 36, 47, 68, 69, 82, 91, 102, and 110. The Psalms of Ascent, 120-134, also known as the Pilgrim Psalms, were sung on the way to the feasts at the temple in Jerusalem.

This volume uses the King James Version of the Bible edited by the author to meet modern prayer needs.

The poetry of the psalms is mainly based on parallelism, not on rhyme. There is a relationship of thought between most sets of two lines.

Poetry Form of PARALLELISM

_____ / A _____ // B

Example:

[A] All Your works give thanks to You O Lord/
[B] and Your godly ones shall bless you// (Ps 145.10)

Poetry Form of CHIASM

A B C
C' B' A'

Example:

[A] *will return* [B] **his mischief** [C]upon his head
[C'] and upon his pate [B'] **violence** [A'] *will descend* (Ps 7.16).

5. Before you Start

Truely, the Psalms could be sung, for they are all songs. As prayers, they are God-inspired essays. Today, and for the next few months, you have the privilege of meditating on and praying some of the most powerful words ever written.

This book is a guide for praying the Psalms.

a. All 150 Psalms are outlined here. For best results, read also other versions of the Psalms as you pray them. Only the 26 main Psalms are presented in this book in full.

b. In order to facilitate personal application in prayer, the Psalms here are presented mainly in the first person rather than the second or third person form.

c. Each Psalm is introduced by an overview in italics that brings some perspective on its content and background. One of the central verses of the Psalm is usually laid out in **bold print** and the number of that verse is given after the title in brackets.

d. Some sections of the Psalms include blank expansions that are there for your notes as you follow the thoughts of the psalmists.

e. Choose one of the five prayer calendars that are suggested in the next pages..

f. Read the Psalm in your own Bible. Then, read-pray the Psalm that is reproduced here.

g. If you do not get out of the Psalms what you expected, it could be that you are in conflict with your God. Pray and find your peace.

6. Overview for Each Psalm

Much of this volume consists of the italic overviews of each of the
150 Psalms. The overviews consist of the Psalm numbers, the
Psalm titles, the Psalm memory verses, and a paragraph presenting
information on the Psalm. That information is not a commentary but
rather an aid in praying the Psalm. Each part is explained here:

a. The numbers of the Psalms are the one presented in the
King James Version of the Bible. While there are other
numbering systems, the one selected is the one generally
used.

b. In the original Hebrew, the Psalms do not have titles. But a
title is useful because it gives a hint as to what follows.
Different authors and Bible translators have developed titles
for each of the Psalms. The ones included in this volume
are the author's effort to relate each Psalm to the prayer life
of the reader.

c. The Psalm memory verse number is again the author's
attempt to focus each Psalm on a particular message.
When the whole Psalm is presented, the memory verse is
in bold print. In some Psalms, there could be more than one
memory verse, but the author has limited them to one
verse.

d. The italic information paragraph usually gives some
background as to the history or use of the Psalm. In many
cases, there could be additional background information,
but these paragraphs were kept short in order to focus on
prayer.

e. Many Psalms consist of a number of parts. Thus the italic
overview often presents these parts with the related verses
in brackets.

f. As you pray each Psalm, check the box next to it. When
you finished them all, start again and also a third time.

7. Psalm Prayer Calendar

There are many ways of praying the Psalms on a regular basis. Choose one or more of the following schedules::

a. **Pray a Psalm a Day:** Read and pray a Psalm a day and include the 22 sections of Psalm 119 on separate days. That makes a total of 171 days or about half a year. You may also paraphrase and write out the psalm. That may be best for individual devotions. For this type, use your own Bible and the overviews for each psalm in this book. Whenever you pray a Psalm, check the box next to that Psalm in this book.

b. **Pray One Main Psalm a Week for 13 weeks from Psalm Books I, II and III:** Read, pray and study well-known Psalms such as Psalms 1, 5, 8, 15, 19, 23, 34, 42, 51, 61, 67, 84 and 86. Consider this also for small group study.

c. **Pray One Main Psalm a Week for 13 weeks from Psalm Books IV and V** such as Psalms 90, 91, 103, 105, 107, 119 (6 parts), 121 and 136. These may be useful for small-group gatherings.

d. **Pray One Memorable Psalms a Week for 20 weeks from these portions:** Psalm 3:3-5, 9:9-11, 13:1-3, 16:5-7, 18:1-3, 25:4-6, 27:4-6, 30:3-5, 32:1-3, 33:18-20, 37:5-7, 53:1-3, 87:4-6, 98:1-3, 111:9-10, 116:15-17, 122:1-3, 127:3-5, 137:3-5, 150:4-6. (The Psalms in schedules b-d are reproduced in full in this book).

e. **Memorize and Do the Psalms:** Memorize the highlighted portion in each Psalm, all the main Psalms, or all the Psalms. Do what the Psalm suggests you should do.

Book One, Creator: Psalm 1-41

1 Living Well (Memory Verse: Psalm 1:2) ☑★☐★☐

To many people, living with a lot of money, power and entertainment means living well. They see fun in doing evil, in harming, in gluttony. They have it all wrong. Living well means to live in harmony with the God of our universe who knows what is best for us and blesses us with His gifts. The psalmist here contrasts what the godly do not do (1), what they do (2-3), and what the godless do (4-6).

1 Blessed am I when I walk not in the counsel of the ungodly, nor stand in the way of sinners, nor sit in the seat of the scornful.

2 But my delight is in the law of the LORD; and in his law do I meditate day and night by *Taking His words into my heart*

3 And I shall be like a tree planted by the rivers of water, that brings forth my fruit in his season; my leaf also shall not wither; and whatsoever I do shall prosper.

4 The ungodly are not so: but are like the chaff which the wind drives away.

5 Therefore the ungodly shall not stand in the judgment, nor sinners in the congregation of the righteous. .

6 For the LORD knows my way that leads to ___*salvation*___ : but the way of the ungodly shall perish.

2 Serve the Lord (2:11). Pray and Read Psalm 2   ☑✱☐✱☐

Jesus will come again--and He warns against rebelling against God.. When He comes, Jesus will receive the earth as an inheritance. Today I can serve Him by respecting Him and helping Him in His mission. That brings real joy. There is a description of the rebellious people, (1-3), the Almighty God (4-6), and the anointed king (7-9).

Open your Bible to Psalm 2, pray the Psalm and read it. Only the main psalms are reproduced in full in this book. The others (like this Psalm 2) are listed, given names, presented in brackets with memory verses, and explained in italic notes. Reproducing all 150 psalms in full would have made too large a book, so this volume features just the main psalms in full and gives helps for the praying of the other psalms. If you do not have a Bible handy, purchase one.

3 The Ladder Up (3:3) ☑★☐★☐

Like David, I am sometimes in the pit of trouble. That may discourage me and appear as if there is no way out (1-2). But as I look to the Lord, I see his ladder that is my way of escape upward. Nothing can stop me in my climb home, no difficulties, nor 10,000 who oppose me. The Lord saves me from the pit of despair and lifts me up (3-8).

3 But you, O LORD, are a shield for me; my glory, and the lifter up of my head when you *console and protect me, and help me see situations from*

4 I cried unto the LORD with my voice, and he heard me out of his *your point of view.* holy hill.

5 I laid me down and slept; I awoke for the LORD sustained me in my difficulties of *fear and despair. I was able to trust God and rely on Him.*

4 Safe in the Lord (4:8) ☑★☐★☐

David was being slandered by his enemies and wanted to know how long that was going to continue (1-2). Even in his distress, he had the assurance that God heard him, put gladness into his heart, and kept him safe (3-8).

5 Praying each Morning (5:3) ☑*□*□

God has a different attitude toward the righteous (11-12) and toward the wicked (4-6, 9). He guides us to know whom we should pray to (1-2), when to pray (3), where to pray (7), and what to pray (8, 10). Our connection with God needs to be reaffirmed each morning.

1 Give ear to my words, O LORD, consider my meditation.

2 Harkin unto the voice of my cry, my King, and my God: for unto you will I pray. (My prayer usually starts with ___Dear Lord___.)

3 My voice shall you hear in the morning, O LORD (usually at ___10:00___ a.m.); each morning will I direct my prayer unto you.

4 For you are not a God that has pleasure in wickedness: neither shall evil dwell with you.

5 The foolish shall not stand in your sight: you hate all workers of iniquity.

6 You shall destroy them that speak falsehood: the LORD will abhor the bloody and deceitful man.

7 But as for me, I will come into your house in the multitude of your mercy: and in your fear will I worship toward your holy temple.

8 Lead me, O LORD, in your righteousness, because of mine enemies; make your way straight before my face.

9 For there is no faithfulness in their mouth; their inward part is very wickedness; their throat is an open grave; they flatter with their tongue.

10 Destroy them, O God; let them fall by their own counsels; cast them out in the multitude of their transgressions; for they have rebelled against thee.

11 But let all those that put their trust in you rejoice: let them ever shout for joy, because you defend them: let them also that love your name be joyful in thee.

12 For you, O Lord, will bless the righteous; with favor you will surround him as with a shield.

6 Lord, Heal Me (6:2) ☑✱☐✱☐

When we come to the Lord, we recognize His power and our weakness. We pray for healing not because we are so good, but because the Lord gives His mercy freely. As we pray, we desire a fast response and often the Lord takes his time. But we do not give up on Him. We know that He hears our prayers and in his good time will act on them. Here we have David's request (1-7) and God's assurance of help (8-10).

7 Falsely Accused (7:17) ☑✱☐✱☐

David was falsely accused by Cush, most likely one of King Saul's lieutenants. David tells of his innocence in the areas of these accusations. He asks God to save him (1-2, 6-9), to examine his motives (3-5), and to protect him (10-16). He knows that God is just and thus he praised Him with song (17).

8 Who Am I? (8:4) ☑*☐*☐

God is infinitely great and man microscopically tiny. But God values us very greatly, gives us opportunities and sheds his amazing glory on us (1-5). He places man in charge of His creation (6-9).

1 O LORD, our Lord, how excellent is your name in all the earth! You have set your glory above the heavens.

2 Out of the mouth of babes and sucklings you have ordained strength because of your enemies, that you might still the enemy and the avenger.

3 When I consider your heavens, the work of your fingers, the moon and the stars, which you have ordained;

4 What is man, that you are mindful of him? and the son of man, that you visit him? *God has made us in His image & likeness*

5 For you have made him a little lower than the angels, and have crowned him with glory and honor by *giving humanity dignity*

6 You made him to have dominion over the works of your hands; you have put all things under his feet:

7 All sheep and oxen, yes, and the beasts of the field;

8 The fowl of the air, and the fish of the sea, and whatsoever passes through the paths of the seas.

9 O LORD our Lord, how excellent is your name in all the earth!

9 My Refuge (9:9) ☑✱☐✱☐

David here possibly celebrates his victory over Goliath and the final victory at the end of time. In times of difficulty, God is the refuge of the oppressed. He helps the helpless and punishes the ungodly. David puts these words into an acrostic based on the first half of the Hebrew alphabet.

9 The LORD also will be a refuge for the oppressed, a refuge from _despair_ **in times of trouble.**

10 And they that know your name will put their trust in you: for you, LORD, have not forsaken them that seek you.

11 Sing praises to the LORD, who dwells in Zion: declare among the people his doings. *Proclaim His marvelous deeds to all the nations...*

10 The Evil King (10:17) ☑✱☐✱☐

In Psalm 10, the psalmist continues the other half of the Hebrew alphabet acrostic that was started in Psalm 9. The palmist describes the evil king, the man of sin, the son of perdition, the man of the earth, who was around at that time but that will be most prominent in the end of time. The wicked oppress the poor, scorn their enemies, boast that they cannot be stopped, curse, threaten, lie and ambush and murder the innocent (1-15). But even with the evil king around, God is the helper of the fatherless and the oppressed. He will bring justice (16-18)

.

11 Mountain Birds (11:1) ☑✱☐✱☐

When in trouble, should we go on in faith or should we fear? In disaster, should we put our trust in the Lord or should we run away to the mountains? (1-3). David here gives guidelines on how to handle the bad headlines of the day, which may include violence, crime, corruption, wars, and unrest. We can rise above these by looking to the Lord (4-7). We reject pessimism and discouragement. We trust the Lord to see us through. The Lord is still in control.

12 God's Words (12:6) ☐✱☐✱☐

We are so privileged to have a record of God's words. We have a written transcription of God's dealing with the ancients. That gives us an idea of how God deals with us as we walk these dusty paths. There is a big contrast between the words of God and the words of men. Man's speech often consists of lies, flattery and two-facedness. Not so with God. David here spells out the problem (1-4), recognizes the Lord's purity (6), and tells of the Lord's protection (5, 7-8).

13 Waiting Time (13:6)   ☐✱☐✱☐

Four times David asks the question How Long? What delays the chariots of God? Why are they so slow? (1-2). David was in deep trouble. He felt that God had forgotten him and had cut him off, he was in a spiritual depression and constantly humiliated. Help was on the way. David here starts with a sigh (1-4) and ends with a song (5-6).

1 How long wilt you forget me, O LORD? Forever? How long will you hide your face from me? _____.

 2 How long shall I take counsel in my soul, having sorrow in my heart daily? How long shall my enemy be exalted over me?

_____.

 3 Consider and hear me, O LORD my God: lighten my eyes, lest I sleep the sleep of death.

14 The Folly of Atheism (14:1)   ☐✱☐✱☐

Saying that there is no God does not make God go away. The fool does not want a God whom he has to obey. Thus he denies his very existence. The fool claims to know all, so he says that God does not exist. The fool claims to exist everywhere, so he claims that God does not exist anywhere. The fool thinks he knows how the earth was formed, but leaves out the designer. Atheists are unwise men that are corrupt and that try to avoid accountability to God. Fools act foolishly (1-5), but the godly have God as refuge (6-7))

15 The People of God (15:1) □✱□✱□

God chooses some people to be his friends. These he permits to live on His holy hill (1). They first have to be born again and then walk in His steps. Genuine faith results in upright living. David here does not paint a full picture of God's people, he just draws a short sketch. He lists integrity, truthfulness (2, 4), avoidance of slander, bribing and harming others as some of the characteristics of God's friends (3, 5). They are comfortable with God and God is comfortable with them.

1 Lord, who shall abide in your tabernacle? who shall dwell in your holy hill? _____.

2 He that walks uprightly, and works righteousness, and speaks the truth in his heart.

3 He that backbites not with his tongue, nor does evil to his neighbor, nor takes up a reproach against his neighbor.

4 In whose eyes a vile person is contemned; but he honors them that fear the LORD. He that swears to his own hurt, and changes not, even when _____.

5 He that puts not out his money to usury, nor takes reward against the innocent. He that does these things shall never be moved.

16 Jesus Lives (16:6) ☐✱☐✱☐

David here describes his confidence in God, his companions and his commitment to God (1-7) He goes on to predict the work of Jesus (8-11). The key to this psalm is the quotation of Peter in Acts 2:25-28. The psalm refers to both the people of God and to Jesus.

5 The LORD is the portion of my inheritance and of my cup: you maintain my lot. **6 The lines are fallen unto me in pleasant places; yes, I have a goodly heritage**.

7 I will bless the LORD, who has given me counsel: my reins also instruct me in the night seasons.

17 The Apple of the Eye (17:8) ☐✱☐✱☐

God's children often suffer seemingly without cause. David asks for justice. He asks to be tested. He asks that God cover him from harm like our eyelids cover our eyes, as a mother-bird protects her young. He calls out for God to hear him (1), vindicate him (2-5), show him love and guard him (5-8), rescue him (9-15) and satisfy him (16).

18 Christ's Early Gospel (18:2) ☐✱☐✱☐

Psalm 18 is a short gospel, telling about the a) death, b) resurrection, c) second coming and d) kingdom of Christ. Each part is well developed and feels like a separate Psalm. Verses 4-19 tell about the death of Jesus Christ, verses 20-30, the resurrection of Christ, verses 31-42, the second coming of Christ, and verses 43-50, the Kingdom of God. This Psalm is intended for both private and public worship.

19 God's Two Books (19:14) ☐✱☐✱☐

God wrote the book of nature (1-6) and inspired the Bible (7-14). These two books are both God's revelation. The book of nature is marred by sin and does not perfectly reflect God's character. But the Bible has been preserved to fully reveal God. Both books give us strength. God is both the creator and the law giver. As such, He is worthy of praise, worship and obedience.

1 The heavens declare the glory of God; and the firmament shows his handy-work.

2 Day unto day utters speech, and night unto night shows knowledge about _____.

3 There is no speech nor language, where their voice is not heard.

4 Their line is gone out through all the earth, and their words to the end of the world. In them he has set a tabernacle for the sun,

5 Which is as a bridegroom coming out of his chamber, and rejoices as a strong man to run a race.

6 His going forth is from the end of the heaven, and his circuit unto the ends of it: and there is nothing hid from the heat thereof.

7 The law of the LORD is perfect, converting the soul: the testimony of the LORD is sure, making wise the simple.

8 The statutes of the LORD are right, rejoicing the heart: the commandment of the LORD is pure, enlightening the eyes.

9 The fear of the LORD is clean, enduring for ever: the judgments of the LORD are true and righteous altogether.

10 More to be desired are they than gold, yes, than much fine gold: sweeter also than honey and the honeycomb.

11 Moreover by them is your servant warned: and in keeping of them there is great reward.

12 Who can understand his errors? Clean me from secret faults like

_____.

13 Keep back your servant also from presumptuous sins; let them not have dominion over me: then shall I be upright, and I shall be innocent from the great transgression.

14 Let the words of my mouth, and the meditation of my heart, be acceptable in your sight, O LORD, my strength, and my redeemer.

20 Help in Trouble (20:7) ☐✱☐✱☐

Before battle, David offered sacrifices to God. He and his people prayed for victory. In God, we too can find help in the day of trouble. We can go forward in the name of the Lord. As king, David makes seven requests from God (1-5, 9) and expresses his confidence in God (6-8).

21 Most Blessed (21:6) ☐✱☐✱☐

Jesus is king of our lives. He is also the one who strengthens us as we fight Satan and move out into mission. Thus we can praise Him for the victory that is ours by faith. We praise Him for the resurrection of Jesus and our future resurrection. In Him, we have life eternal. The Lord gives David and us the desire of our hearts (2-12) and we give Him our devotions (1, 13)

22 The Suffering of Jesus (22:10) ☐✱☐✱☐

Jesus suffered more than any man. And we too, like David, may have a time of suffering. We realize that we, like Jesus, are in a battle between good and evil. At times it appears that the wrong side is winning. But as we trust the Lord, He eventually brings us to victory. The suffering (1-8, 12-18) ends in a glorious coronation (22-31).

23 The Good Shepherd (23:4) ☐✱☐✱☐

This psalm is for people who accept Jesus as their personal Shepherd. It is for believers who trust Jesus to provide all they need (not want). Those who do so shall not lack food, refreshment, vitality, nor moral direction. The promise of not fearing evil is one that gives us courage to face the greatest obstacles. The Lord is my shepherd (1-4), guide (3-4), and healer (5-6) Annie Flint wrote: "His love has no limit, His grace has no measure, His power has no boundaries known unto men, For out of His infinite riches in Jesus, He gives, and gives, and gives again".

1 The LORD is my shepherd; I shall not want. I have all I need in

_____ .

2 He makes me to lie down in green pastures: he leads me beside the still waters.

3 He restores my soul: he leads me in the paths of righteousness for his name's sake.

4 Yes, though I walk through the valley of the shadow of death, I will fear no evil: for you are with me; your rod and your staff they comfort me. I fear no evil when _____ .

5 You prepare a table before me in the presence of mine enemies: you anoint my head with oil; my cup runs over.

6 Surely goodness and mercy shall follow me all the days of my life: and I will dwell in the house of the LORD forever.

24 The King of Glory (24:3) ☐✶☐✶☐

Like in Psalm 15, the question starts with "who". Are you included among the people with clean hands and a pure heart"? You may think of the removal of the ark or the second coming of Jesus. I find here the glorious kingdom (1-6) and the glorious King (7-10).

25 The Way (25:4) ☐✶☐✶☐

This Psalm of David is a blend of a prayer for deliverance, forgiveness and guidance. David asks here to be protected (1-3, 15-22), piloted (4-5, 8-10), pardoned (6-7. 11), and prospered (12-14). This is an acrostic psalm, starting each verse with one of the 22 letters of the Hebrew alphabet.

4 Show me your ways, O LORD; teach me your paths.

5 Lead me in your truth, and teach me: for you are the God of my salvation; on you do I wait all the day.

6 Remember, O LORD, your tender mercies and your loving kindnesses; for they have been ever of old.

26 Integrity (26:2) ☐✶☐✶☐

David has been accused falsely. He asks God to clean his record. The reasons that he gives are that he has trusted the Lord (1), has lived according to the truth (2-3, 11), refused fellowship with the ungodly (4-5, 9-10), and walked in integrity (11-12).

27 Wait Without Fear (27:4)   ☐*☐*☐

Jesus did not fear when he was arrested and brought to trial. We too can face our trials without fear in the strength of the Lord (1-3). Sometimes we have to wait awhile before help arrives. But if we go by faith, help will arrive. David makes three requests of the Lord: to worship in God's house (4-6), to be close to the Lord (7-10) and to receive God's help (11-14)

4 One thing have I desired of the LORD, that will I seek after; that I may dwell in the house of the LORD all the days of my life, to behold the beauty of the LORD, and to enquire in his temple.
About what? _____.

5 For in the time of trouble he shall hide me in his pavilion: in the secret of his tabernacle shall he hide me; he shall set me up upon a rock. which is _____.

6 And now shall mine head be lifted up above mine enemies round about me: therefore will I offer in his tabernacle sacrifices of joy; I will sing, yes, I will sing praises unto the LORD.

28 The Lord Hears. (28:7)   ☐*☐*☐

Sometimes it appears that God is like a silent rock that does not respond to our pleading. He may be silent because He loves us, or He tests us, or because we cannot hear Him when He speaks. He is a living rock that anchors our souls. God is worth waiting for. David depended on the Lord (1-5) and delighted in Him (6-9).

29 The Lord's Voice (29:2) ☐✱☐✱☐

To David, the voice of the Lord was like storm and thunder. There are three parts to this Psalm. The first is a beautiful call to worship (1-2), The second part gives seven examples of the power of the Lord's voice in nature (3-9). The third part describes Noah during and after the flood (10-11). The voice of the Lord is powerful.

30 The Healer (30:5) ☐✱☐✱☐

The Lord is our healer and helper. We thank and praise Him for His healing and help. David prayed this prayer at the dedication of the temple. He praised God for victory over danger, disease and death (1-3), for the shortness of weeping (4, 5) and help in trouble (6-10).The Lord turns our mourning into dancing (11-12).

3 O LORD, you have brought up my soul from the grave: you have kept me alive, that I should not go down to the pit.

4 Sing unto the LORD, O you saints of his, and give thanks at the remembrance of his holiness.

5 For his anger endures but a moment; in his favor is life: weeping may endure for a night, but joy comes in the morning when _____ .

31 Into Your Hands. (31:5)   □✱□✱□

Jesus knew this Psalm by heart. At His death, Jesus used this prayer for deliverance (5). David asks the Lord for deliverance (1-5), he shares his downs (9-13) and his ups (14-19), his concerns with suffering and the resurrection (20-24). God encourages us.

32 Forgiven (32:5)   □✱□✱□

Forgiveness frees us from the burden of sin. It removes guilt and debts. As we acknowledge our sins, God forgives them. Forgiveness brings peace and joy. The Psalm consists of a discussion of confession (1-5), advice on repentance (6-7), and guidance to live a godly life (8-11). This psalm is similar to Psalm 51.

1 Blessed is he whose transgression is forgiven, whose sin is covered.

2 Blessed is the man to whom the LORD imputes not iniquity, and in whose spirit there is no guile.

3 When I kept silence, my bones waxed old through my roaring all the day long.

33 Primer of Praise (33:18)　☐✱☐✱☐

This Psalm outlines ways to praise the Lord and ends with a group response of praise. We have so much to praise the Lord for. We praise God with joy and song (1-3). We praise Him for His goodness, power, sovereignty, omniscience, and protection (4-22).

18 Behold, the eyes of the LORD are upon them that fear him, upon them that hope in his mercy;

19 To deliver their soul from death, and to keep them alive in famine.

20 Our soul waits for the LORD: he is our help and our shield.

34 Free from Fear (34:7)   □✹□✹□

This salvation psalm is an acrostic based on the events of 1 Samuel 21:10-14. When we respect (fear) the Lord, we can live without fear. That is real freedom. David is both learner (1-7) and teacher (8-22).

1 I will bless the LORD at all times: his praise shall continually be in my mouth.

2 My soul shall make her boast in the LORD: the humble shall hear thereof, and be glad.

3 O magnify the LORD with me, and let us exalt his name together.

4 I sought the LORD, and he heard me, and delivered me from all my fears.

5 They looked unto him, and were lightened: and their faces were not ashamed.

6 This poor man cried, and the LORD heard him, and saved him out of all his troubles.

7 The angel of the LORD encamps round about them that fear him, and delivers them.

8 O taste and see that the LORD is good: blessed is the man that trusts in him.

9 O fear the LORD: for there is no want to them that fear him.

10 The young lions do lack, and suffer hunger: but they that seek the LORD shall not want any good thing.

11 Come, you children unto me: I will teach you the fear of the LORD.

12 What man is he that desires life, and loves many days, that he may see good?_____.

13 Keep your tongue from evil, and your lips from speaking guile.
14 Depart from evil, and do good; seek peace, and pursue it.

15 The eyes of the LORD are upon the righteous, and his ears are open unto their cry.

16 The face of the LORD is against them that do evil, to cut off the remembrance of them from the earth.

17 The righteous cry, and the LORD hears, and delivers them out of all their troubles.

18 The LORD is nigh unto them that are of a broken heart; and saves such as be of a contrite spirit.

19 Many are the afflictions of the righteous: but the LORD delivers him out of them all at the time of _____..

20 He keeps all his bones: not one of them is broken.

21 Evil shall slay the wicked: and they that hate the righteous shall be desolate.

22 The LORD redeems the soul of his servants: and none of them that trust in him shall be desolate.

35 Friends and Traitors (35:9) □✱□✱□

David had both good friends and evil traitors. He blesses his friends and asks God to deal with the traitors. He asked God to protect him (1-10), to reward him (11-18), and to vindicate him (19-28).

36 The Evil and the Good (36:9) □✱□✱□

David here highlights the reality of evil. He contrasts evil (1-4) and good (5-12). He asks God to bless the godly and humble the godless. He lists some six characteristics of God. We praise our good God.

37 Trust the Lord (37:5) □✱□✱□

This is an acrostic about the evil prospering and the good suffering. David here listed some 11 things the godly sow and 14 things they reap. Then he lists two things the godless sow and seven things they reap. The difference between the evil and good is seen at the end.

5 Commit your way unto the LORD; trust also in him; and he shall bring it to pass.

6 And he shall bring forth your righteousness as the light, and your judgment as the noonday.

7 Rest in the LORD, and wait patiently for him: fret not yourself because of him who prospers in his way, because of the man who brings wicked devices to pass.

38 Sorrow for Sin (38:15) ☐✻☐✻☐

David remembers his sin and struggles with the memory. Then there is Jesus who suffered for David's and our sins. Both went through great physical and mental distress. David presents the penalty for sin (1-14) and his pardon (15-22). We depend on the Lord for His pardon.

39 From Despondent to Confident (39:12) ☐✻☐✻☐

David realized that he was in difficulty. He asks how long trouble would follow him. He hoped it is over. He described his own silence (1-3), his despondency (4-6), and lastly his confidence and repentance (7-13). In the last two sections David asked the Lord to show him the frailty of life, to save him, to spare him, and to satisfy him. God is compassionate.

40 Rescued (40:5) ☐✻☐✻☐

David praised God for what He has done (1-5) and what He desires (6-10). Then David prays for rescue from his troubles and from his enemies (11-17). This Psalm also deals with the resurrection of Jesus. Thank God that Jesus was resurrected. Psalm 40:13-17 is also in Psalm 70 and we will deal with it there.

. 41 Without Health (41:4) ☐✻☐✻☐

Those who help the poor, receive from God protection, prosperity, help in sickness and forgiveness (1-4.) God is faithful (5-13). David was sick and his enemies hoped he would die. But he trusted God to heal him.

Book Two, Rescuer: Psalm 42-72

42 The Depressed (42:5) ☐✱☐✱☐

The spiritually depressed can find healing in God. Jesus also wept. Notice David's desire (1-2), his despair (3, 9-10), and his determination (4-8, 11).

1 As the hart pants after the water brooks, so pants my soul after you, O God. **2** My soul thirsts for God, for the living God: when shall I come and appear before God? .

3 My tears have been my meat day and night, while they continually say unto me, Where is your God?_____.

4 When I remember these things, I pour out my soul in me: for I had gone with the multitude, I went with them to the house of God, with the voice of joy and praise, with a multitude that kept the holy day.

5 Why are you cast down, O my soul? And why are you sad? Hope in God: for I shall yet praise him for the help of his face.

6 O my God, my soul is cast down within me: therefore will I remember you from the land of Jordan, and of the Hermonites, from the hill Mizar.

7 Deep calls unto deep at the noise of you waterspouts: all your waves and your billows are gone over me.

8 Yet the LORD will command his loving kindness in the day time, and in the night his song shall be with me, and my prayer unto the God of my life.

9 I will say unto God my rock, Why have you forgotten me? Why go I mourning because of the oppression of the enemy?_____.

10 As with a sword in my bones, my enemies reproach me while they say daily to me: Where is your God?

11 Why are you cast down, O my soul, and why are you troubled in me? Hope in God, for I shall yet praise Him, who is the health of my face, and my God.

43 Light Leads (43:5) ☐✻☐✻☐

This psalm seems to be connected to Psalm 42. Psalm 42:5 and 11 are repeated in Psalm 43:5. There is a progression as the sons of Korah pray and worship on the holy hills, at the tabernacle, before God, their exceeding joy. The psalmist asked God to defend him (1-2). God's light can lead out of spiritual depression (3-5)

44 God Helps (44:22) ☐✱☐✱☐

*This is a praise song to God and a lament. God, You have helped.
You are not helping. You should help. You will help (:1, 9, 17, 23).
The Psalm deals with Israel's past glory (1-8) and Israel's present
grief (9-26.)*

45 Christ and His Church(45:7) ☐✱☐✱☐

*This Psalm praised the king at his wedding. Christ is the King, and
His bride is the church. The king returns at the Second Advent. And
in Psalm 45:6, God addresses his Son as God. The Psalm describes
the king's five characteristics (1-8) and the clothing, commitment and
coming glory of the bride (9-17). Christ and His church are closely
connected.*

46 My Refuge (46:10) ☐✱☐✱☐

*We have nothing to fear. The Lord reigns, we have peace in Him.
God protects us (1-3). He is the God of the paradise (4-5), power (6-
8), peace (9), and praise (10-11). This Psalm, and the next two,
relate to the time when Hezekiah was king.*

47 The Awesome King (47:2) ☐✱☐✱☐

*The Messiah is king. We praise Him. He gave Hezekiah's general a
glorious victory over the Assyrians. He also gives us victory. The
Lord most high is truly awesome (2)*

48 Celebrate (48:11)　□*□*□

The Lord watches over Jerusalem. He also watches over us. Parts of the Psalm describe the God of Jerusalem, the other parts the Jerusalem of God. Each of these two sections has four parts. Three times Jerusalem is here called Mount Zion, the city of our God.

49 Wealth and Death (49:15) □*□*□

The psalmist calls on all to listen to his wisdom (1-5). The wealth of the evil will fail them. God is just. Wait and trust him. Do not trust riches, all will be left behind. We cannot take any material things with us, only who we are. We cannot avoid death (6-14, 17-20) Our Savior will rescue us from the power of death (15-16)

50 The Judgment (50:14)　□*□*□

The setting here is a courtroom with God as judge, Israel as the defendant and heaven and earth the witness. There is a description of the judge (1-3, 6), the judged (4-5, 7) and the judgment (8-23). The judgment part is divided into what God desires, what He despises, and what he declares.

51 Confession (51:10) □✱□✱□

This is David's confession when Nathan exposes David's sin with Bathsheba. 2 Sam 12. He asked for mercy (1, 2) recognized his sin (3-6), prayed for a clean heart (7-12) and promised to teach, sing and praise God (13-15). He realized that God desires a broken and repentant heart (16-19). He let God turn his life around.

1 Have mercy upon me, O God, according to your loving kindness: according unto the multitude of your tender mercies blot out my transgressions by _____..

2 Wash me thoroughly from my iniquity, and cleanse me from my sin.

3 For I acknowledge my transgressions: and my sin is ever before me.

4 Against you, you only, have I sinned, and done this evil in your sight: that you might be justified when you speak, and be clear when you judge.

5 Behold, I was shaped in iniquity; and in sin did my mother conceive me.

6 Behold, you desire truth in the inward parts: and in the hidden part you shall make me to know wisdom.

7 Purge me with hyssop, and I shall be clean: wash me, and I shall be whiter than snow.

8 Make me to hear joy and gladness; that the bones which you have broken may rejoice.

9 Hide your face from my sins, and blot out all my iniquities.

10 Create in me a clean heart, O God; and renew a right spirit within me, now that _____.

11 Cast me not away from your presence; and take not your Holy Spirit from me.

12 Restore unto me the joy of your salvation; and uphold me with your free spirit.

13 Then will I teach transgressors your ways; and sinners shall be converted unto you.

14 Deliver me from blood guiltiness, O God, God of my salvation: and my tongue shall sing aloud of your righteousness.

15 O Lord, open my lips; and my mouth shall show forth your praise.

16 For you desire not sacrifice; else would I give it: you delight not in burnt offering.

17 The sacrifices of God are a broken spirit: a broken and a contrite heart, O God, you will not despise.

18 Do good in your good pleasure unto Zion: build the walls of Jerusalem.

19 Then shall you be pleased with the sacrifices of righteousness, with burnt offering and whole burnt offering: then shall they offer bullocks upon your altar.

52 The Traitor (52:8) ☐✱☐✱☐

This psalm is based on Doeg, the Edomite, in 1 Samuel 21 and 22. First, Doeg's character is described, then his doom. The psalm ends with David praising God. There is a contrast of the boast of the godless (1-5) and the boast of the godly (6-9).

53 The Ignorant Atheist (53:6) ☐✱☐✱☐

Atheists are people without God., that deny the very existence of God. The fool is not necessarily stupid or crazy. He may be intelligent or brilliant. But he does not accept the evidence as to the creative power of God. He is willfully ignorant. This psalm is very similar to Psalm 14. God's name in the first line is Jehovah, in the second Elohim. There is a clear separation between God's foolish foes (1-5) and His faithful friends (6).

1 The fool has said in his heart, there is no God. Corrupt are they, and have done abominable iniquity: there is none that do good.

2 God looked down from heaven upon the children of men, to see if there were any that did understand, that did seek God.

3 Every one of them is gone back: they are altogether become filthy; there is none that doeth good, no, not one.

54 Safe in Danger (54:4)　□✱□✱□

David was suffering because of the betrayal of Ziphites as recorded in 1 Samuel 23:19. This may be an appropriate prayer when people suffer. God is our helper. David is in trouble (1-3), trusts God (4), and will triumph (6-7).

55 Handling Problems (55:22)　□✱□✱□

David trusted God whatever the circumstances. We can too. Besieged by foes and betrayed by friends (2-15, 20-21), David nevertheless trusts God to save him (16-19, 22-23).

56 From Fear to Faith (56:8)　□✱□✱□

In fear, David took refuge among the Philistines (1 Samuel 21). In faith he prayed. Here he recounts the actions of his foes (1-2, 5-6) and of his friends (3-4, 7-13).

57 Safe in a Cave. (57:1)　□✱□✱□

David was hiding from Saul (1 Samuel 22). He cried out for God's mercy and protection (1-3). His enemies have set a trap for him (4,6). He is safe in a cave. He praised God and thanked Him (5, 7-11).

58 Evil Judges (58:11)　□✱□✱□

The Lord and David are troubled by unjust judges and people. David cried out against the godless (1-9) and about the reward of the godly (10-11). The victors walk the battlefield. (10).

59 God Delivers (59:16)   □✶□✶□

Saul chased David, but God looked after him and delivered him (1 Sam 19:11). God was his refuge. Again David described his foes (1-7, 11-15) and his friends (8-10, 16-17)

60 Hope in Victory (60:11)   □✶□✶□

David's kingdom was invaded, but he was encouraged and enabled. First David asks God why He rejected His people (1-5, 10-12) and then he asks God for help (5-12). Final victory is certain.

61 Jesus, the Rock (61:2) □✶□✶□

David's heart was overwhelmed. But soon he changes from distress to praise. God was still there for him. David asked God to lead Him (1-5), and to lengthen his life (6-8).

1 Hear my cry, O God; attend unto my prayer.

2 From the end of the earth will I cry unto you, when my heart is overwhelmed: lead me to the rock that is higher than I which is _____.

3 For you have been a shelter for me, and a strong tower from the enemy at _____.

4 I will abide in your tabernacle forever: I will trust in the covert of your wings. .

5 For you, O God, have heard my vows: you have given me the heritage of those that fear your name.

6 You will prolong the king's life: and his years as many generations.

7 He shall abide before God forever: O prepare mercy and truth, which may preserve him.

8 So will I sing praise unto your name forever, that I may daily perform my vows.

62 Only God (62:7) ☐✶☐✶☐

Only God is the true refuge .Here is a short description of the evil (3-4). We are reminded that God is with those who trust Him and the faithful (1-2, 5-10). God reaches out to us and rewards us (11-12).

63 My Soul Thirsts (63:1) ☐✶☐✶☐

David's soul thirsted and longed for God early in life and early each day (1-2). He praised and blessed God (3-7). God delivered him and destroyed his enemies (8-11). Three times David starts a verse with the words "my soul."

64 Survivors (64:10) ☐✶☐✶☐

David describes two archery contests. The great enemy is fear. David asked for protection (1-6). God answers and the good survive.(7-10).

65 The Second Advent (65:4) ☐✶☐✶☐

The final harvest is at the second coming of Christ. God forgives. God provides. God saves. David thanked God for redemption (1-5) and His creation. (6-13).

66 The Lord's Prayer (66:5) ☐✶☐✶☐

At the very end, all the world will worship God. We now worship God who tests us and delivers us. Come, see, hear. We praise God for His deeds (1-12) and dedicate ourselves to serve Him (13-20).

67 Mission Call (67:2) ☐✱☐✱☐

The good news is to go to all nations. We are all missionaries. God's glory is seen among God's people and among the gentiles (1-5). God gives both material and spiritual blessings (6-7). Note the five times that the word "let" is used.

1 God be merciful unto us, and bless us; and cause your face to shine upon us.

2 That your way may be known upon earth, your saving health among all nations when _____.

3 Let the people praise you, O God; let all the people praise you.

4 O let the nations be glad and sing for joy: for you shall judge the people righteously, and govern the nations upon earth.

5 Let the people praise you, O God; let all the people praise you.

6 Then shall the earth yield her increase; and God, even our own God, shall bless us.

7 God shall bless us; and all the ends of the earth shall fear him and
_____ .

68 The Journey of the Ark (68:19)　□✱□✱□

This seven-part psalm traces the ark on its journey from the wilderness to its resting place in Jerusalem. When it moved, God moved. You may also look at it as the journey of Jesus to Calvary. In some way, it may also be part of our own spiritual journey home.

Verses 1-6 are an introductory hymn, verses 7-9 are about the ark in the wilderness, verses 10-14 about the ark in Canaan, verses 15-19 about David capturing Jerusalem, verses 20-23 about the victory of the Jesubites, verses 24-27 about the ark in Jerusalem, and verses 28-35 about the final victory of God/

69 The Sorrow of Jesus (69:30)　□✱□✱□

David walked with us through the suffering and death of Jesus. Also, in verses 1-18 David asks the Lord to save him, in verses 19-29, to judge his enemies, and in verses 30-36 that he be glorified. A special beautiful prayer for four things is in verses 16-18.

70 Hasten to Help. (70:4)　□✱□✱□

This Psalm is mainly a copy of Psalm 40:13-17. It is a prayer for help against persecutors. There is an urgency in this plea. The word "hasten" is used three times.

71 Change (71:18)　□✱□✱□

God helps us now (1-4), he helped us in the past (5-13) and will help in the future and in old age (14-24). This psalm is also a prayer for the remnant. In verses 3-7 is a list of five affirmations starting with "you are."

72 The Coming Judge (72:4) ☐✶☐✶☐

Jesus, at his second coming, will usher in the golden era of peace. Solomon here writes about God's impartial judgments, His universal dominion, His compassionate reign and His prosperity. He lists the characteristics of the good King ((1-17) and praises the Lord (18-19).

Book Three, Deliverer: 73-89

73   The Dilemma of Faith (73:17)   ☐✶☐✶☐

The psalmist Asaph is here writing about his dilemma of faith. He challenges the doubter, the wrestler with evil, the worshipper of good, and the conqueror. Verses 2-16 are about the prosperity of the wicked, verse 17-28 about the author's changed view on that subject

74 The Destruction of the Temple (74:12)   ☐✶☐✶☐

This lament reminds the Lord to remember His temple that has been damaged (1-12). Asaph reminds the Lord that He is His King and Creator with nine sentences starting with "You." (13-17). He asks the Lord to rescue His people and to remember His promises (18-23).

75 Thanks (75:1)   ☐✶☐✶☐

This Psalm is one of thanks. Psalm 75 answers Psalm 74. Jesus speaks, He will return and punish the wicked. There are five sentences that start with the word "I" and that describe what God will do (2-4, 9).

76 Protection (76:11)   ☐✱☐✱☐

God lives in Jerusalem gloriously and strong (1-10,12) Bring presents to the Lord (11). The Lord's angels saved Jerusalem when the Assyrian army attacked.

77 From Distress to Delight (77:12)   ☐✱☐✱☐

Asaph here sighs, sinks, sings, and soars (1-10). God heals our stress. In verses 7-9 are five rhetorical questions that can be answered with "no." Verses 16-20 describe Israel's wonderful passage through the Red Sea.

78 History (78:35)   ☐✱☐✱☐

Learn from the past, so that you will not make the same mistakes as those before you. God is the best master to serve. Verses 1-11 features the giving of the law, verses 12-39 Egypt and the wilderness, verses 40-53 the plagues, verses 54-67 the promised land and verses 68-72 Mt Zion. Here are recounted some ten ways God helped His people in spite their rebellion.

79 In Trouble (79:9)   ☐✱☐✱☐

In this parallel to Psalm 74, Asaph here describes the destruction of Jerusalem and the temple (1-4). He asks the Lord to forgive, to help, to avenge, and he promised that he will thank and praise God forever (5-13).

80 Restore Us (80:3)   □*□*□

God's people are like a flock (1-7) and like a vineyard (8-16). The Psalm ends with a plea for revival and restoration (17-19). Three times Asaph repeats the same verse and pleads to be restored (3, 7, 19). We all need restoration.

81 The Feast of Trumpets (81:10)   □*□*□

The Jews saw the Feast Day of Trumpets as a judgment day when all Israel passed before the Lord. This psalm was sung on that day. Verses 1-3 list four musical instruments. We need to rejoice in the Lord (1-4), remember the Lord (5-7), and listen and obey (8-16).

82 Judges on Trial (82:3)   □*□*□

God judges the judges of the world (1) and finds them unfaithful. The Psalm describes the judge's work (2-4), their ignorance (5), and their fragility (6-8). The term "gods" may be also translated here as "judges." The Psalm ends with a request for God to judge the world.

83 Victory in Jesus (83:18)   □*□*□

Israel was besieged many times (1-4). Recently it was at their declaration of independence on May 15, 1948 and during the six-day war in May, 1967. Many times, the old and modern Israelites asked for victory and God rescued them (9-18). God's people too will be victorious. God still rules the world.

84 Heading Home (84:10) □✱□✱□

This psalm may express the longing of the exiles to be at the temple in Jerusalem, or of Christians seeking fellowship, or of pilgrims homesick for heaven. The desire of the pilgrim is to be near the temple (1-3). What fellowship are you seeking? Are you going from strength to strength? God is full of grace and delight (4-12)

1 How amiable are your tabernacles, O LORD of hosts!

2 My soul longs, yes, even faints for the courts of the LORD: my heart and my flesh cries out for the living God.

3 Yea, the sparrow has found a house, and the swallow a nest for herself, where she may lay her young, even your altars, O LORD of hosts, my King, and my God.

4 Blessed are they that dwell in your house: they will be praising you in _____.

5 Blessed is the man whose strength is in you; in whose heart are the ways of them.

6 Who passing through the valley of Baca (means weeping) make it a well; the rain also fills the pools.

7 They go from strength to strength, every one of them in Zion appears before God to _____.

8 O LORD God of hosts, hear my prayer: give ear, O God of Jacob.

9 Behold, O God our shield, and look upon the face of your anointed.

10 For a day in your courts is better than a thousand. I would rather be a doorkeeper in the house of my God, than to dwell in the tents of wickedness.

11 For the LORD God is a sun and shield: the LORD will give grace and glory: no good thing will he withhold from them that walk uprightly,

12 O LORD of hosts, blessed is the man that trusts in you.

85 Revive Us (85:2)   ☐✱☐✱☐

Consider the past revivals. Also consider the plea and the promise for revival. The Lord restores the depressed. In verses 4-7, the word "us" is repeated 6 times. We move with God from the past (1-3), to the present (4-7) and on into the future (8-13).

86 Reasonable Prayers (86:4) ☐✷☐✷☐

David petitions and adores God and then adds reasons for them. Eight of the reasons start with the word "for" (1-13).Then are listed five of God's characteristics (15). David asks for a sign that things will turn out well and that the Lord will help (16-18).

1 Bow down your ear, O LORD, hear me: for I am poor and needy.

2 Preserve my soul; for I am holy: O you my God, save your servant that trusts in you.

3 Be merciful to me, O Lord: for I cry to you daily at _____.

4 Rejoice the soul of your servant: for to you, O Lord, do I lift up my soul in that _____.

5 For you, Lord, are good, and ready to forgive; and plenteous in mercy unto all them that call upon you.

6 Give ear, O LORD, unto my prayer; and attend to the voice of my supplications.

7 In the day of my trouble I will call upon you: for you will answer me.

8 Among the gods there is none like unto you, O Lord; neither are there any works like unto your works.

9 All nations whom you have made shall come and worship before you, O Lord; and shall glorify your name.

10 For you are great, and do wondrous things: you are God alone.

11 Teach me your way, O LORD; I will walk in your truth: unite my heart to fear your name.

12 I will praise you, O Lord my God, with all my heart: and I will glorify your name for evermore.

13 For great is your mercy toward me: and you have delivered my soul from the lowest hell.

14 O God, the proud are risen against me, and the assemblies of violent men have sought after my soul; and have not set you before them.

15 But you, O Lord, are a God full of compassion, and gracious, long suffering, and plenteous in mercy and truth.

16 O turn to me, and have mercy upon me; give your strength to your servant, and save the son of your handmaid.

17 Show me a token for good; that they which hate me may see it, and be ashamed: because you, LORD, have helped me, and comforted me.

87 God's Census (87:6) ☐✻☐✻☐

Jerusalem is God's special city because he chose it for himself (1-3). It commands no harbor, no river, no major highway. It is an honor to be a citizen of physical or spiritual Jerusalem (4-7). God records the birthplaces of his people and considers them.

4 I will make mention of Rahab (Egypt) and Babylon to them that know me: behold Philistia, and Tyre, with Ethiopia; this man was born there. 5 And of Zion it shall be said, This and that man was born in her: and the highest himself shall establish her.

 6 The LORD shall count, when he writes up the people, that this man was born there.

88 Nearly Hopeless (88:13) ☐✻☐✻☐

This psalm is a lamentation full of sadness, gloom, bitterness and sorrow. The suffering is because of unanswered prayers (1-2, 13), unending pain and trouble (3-5, 9, 15) and undeserved persecution (6-8, 10-12, 14, 16-18). But keep on praying. God hears.

89 The Covenant with David (89:15) ☐✻☐✻☐

Ethan here describes God's covenant with David and his descendants. Each of the four sections of this psalm deals with a different action we can have toward God. Verses 15-18 presents a New Year Prayer. Faith triumphs. Verses 1-18 encourage us to praise God, verses 19-37 to trust God, verses 38-45 to complain to God, and verses 46-52 to wait for God.

Book Four, Protector: Psalm 90-106

90 A Time for Graves (90:10)　☐✱☐✱☐

Nearly all the children of Israel who had left Egypt died before they reached the Promised Land. Here Moses contemplates their graves. Some consider this the oldest of the Psalms. God's and man's perspectives of time are presented in verses 4 and 10. The eternity of the Creator (1-4) is contrasted with the mortality of men (5-17). Few live past the eighty years that is here suggested (10). Moses asks us to number our days and appreciate each one.(12)

1 Lord, you have been our dwelling place in all generations.

2 Before the mountains were brought forth, or ever you had formed the earth and the world, even from everlasting to everlasting, you are God.

3 You turned man to destruction; and said, Return, you children of men.

4 For a thousand years in your sight are but as yesterday when it is past, and as a watch in the night. So _____.

5 You carried them away as with a flood; they are as a sleep: in the morning they are like grass which grows up.

6 In the morning it flourishes, and grows up; in the evening it is cut down, and withers.

7 For we are consumed by your anger, and by your wrath are we troubled.

8 You have set our iniquities before you, our secret sins in the light of your countenance.

9 For all our days are passed away in your wrath: we spend our years as a tale that is told.

10 The days of our years are threescore years and ten; and if by reason of strength they be fourscore years, yet is their strength labor and sorrow; for it is soon cut off, and we fly away. But _____.

11 Who knows the power of your anger? even according to your fear, so is your wrath.

12 So teach us to number our days, that we may apply our hearts to wisdom.

13 Return, O LORD, how long? and have compassion on your servants.

14 O satisfy us early with your mercy; that we may rejoice and be glad all our days.

15 Make us glad according to the days wherein you have afflicted us, and the years wherein we have seen evil.

16 Let your work appear unto your servants, and your glory unto their children.

17 And let the beauty of the LORD our God be upon us: and establish the work of our hands upon us; yes, establish the work of our hands.

91 Christ and I, the Victors (91:15) ☐✸☐✸☐

This psalm is about Jesus. But it also promises us God's protection and victory. It presents much encouragement to us. On his 100th birthday, George Couran recited this psalm from memory before an Orangevale, California church congregation. Presented here are the foundation and foes of faith (1-3), the fruits of faith (4-10, 13), the friends of faith (11-12), and the fellowship of faith (14-16).

1 He that dwells in the secret place of the most High shall abide under the shadow of the Almighty.

2 I will say of the LORD, He is my refuge and my fortress: my God; in him will I trust.

3 Surely he shall deliver you from the snare of the fowler, and from the noisome pestilence.

4 He shall cover you with his feathers, and under his wings shall you trust: his truth shall be your shield and buckler.

5 You shall not be afraid of the terror by night; nor of the arrow that flies by day; nor _____.

6 Nor for the pestilence that walk in darkness; nor for the destruction that wastes at noonday.

7 A thousand shall fall at your side, and ten thousand at your right hand; but it shall not come near you.

8 Only with your eyes shall you behold and see the reward of the wicked.

9 Because you have made the LORD, who is my refuge, even the most High, your habitation;

10 There shall no evil befall you, neither shall any plague come near your dwelling, nor _____.

11 For he shall give his angels charge over you, to keep you in all your ways.

12 They shall bear you up in their hands, lest you dash your foot against a stone.

13 You shall tread upon the lion and adder: the young lion and the dragon you shall trample under feet.

14 Because he has set his love upon me, therefore will I deliver him: I will set him on high, because he has known my name.

15 He shall call upon me, and I will answer him: I will be with him in trouble; I will deliver him, and honor him.

16 With long life will I satisfy him, and show him my salvation.

92 We Flourish (92:4) ☐✱☐✱☐

This psalm is a Sabbath song and prayer in praise of God. In spiritual botany, the evil are grass (6-7, 9) and the good evergreens (1-5, 8, 10-15). Even in old age, we can bear fruit (14). We are blessed as we consider His ways.

93 Christ Reigns (93:1) ☐✱☐✱☐

This song is ready for the crowning of Jesus as Lord of Lords. The exiles return home. That is glorious. The psalm describes the Lord's robes (1), His reign (2-4) and His righteousness (5).

94 Why the Godly Suffer (94:12) ☐✱☐✱☐

There is much injustice in this world. How long will it continue? (1-7) We are asked to accept God's warning (8-11), His discipline (12-15) and then work for justice (16-23). The psalm contains four questions and the given answers help us understand suffering.

95 Call to Worship (95:6) ☐✱☐✱☐

The Holy Spirit calls us to worship. This is how you do it. Remember the positive praise (1-7) and avoid the negative rebellion (8-11) that gets terrible results). This Psalm was often used at the celebration of the Feast of the Tabernacles.

96 Worship the Lord (96:9)   ☐✻☐✻☐

We are here asked to worship and praise the Lord in many ways. Singing seems to be always a part of that worship. But the singing should be from the heart, expressing a worshipful inner attitude. This is a call to witnessing (1-6, 10), to worship (7-9) and to celebration (11-13)

97 Enjoy God's Light (97:11)   ☐✻☐✻☐

Jesus takes his throne. He brings light into our hearts. He's exalted. And fire burns up the corrupt (3). They are no more. The Psalm ends with a description of what the Lord does for His people (10-12)

98 Sing to the Lord (98:4)   ☐✻☐✻☐

Christ Returns. It is time to celebrate with a new song his glorious coming. He is the answer to our prayers, to our expectations. He tells us what to sing (1), why to sing (2-3, 7-8), and when to sing (9)

1 O sing unto the LORD a new song; for he has done marvelous things: his right hand, and his holy arm, have gotten him the victory.

2 The LORD has made known his salvation: his righteousness has he openly shown in the sight of the heathen in _____.

3 He has remembered his mercy and his truth toward the house of Israel: all the ends of the earth have seen the salvation of our God.

99 God is Holy (99:5)   □✱□✱□

God is totally different from us. He is holy. That fact is presented three times in this psalm (3, 5, 9). He is supreme and sinless. As we trust Him, some of his holiness is reflected on us.

100 Thanksgiving (100:4)   □✱□✱□

With joy, submit to God and thank Him. He is our Song, Creator, Shepherd, Blessed One, and Love (1-5). We move from joy to submission to heartfelt thanks. This is a good psalm to pray on Thanksgiving Day.

101 The Faithful (101:6)   □✱□✱□

Here is a contrast between the faithful (1-2, 6) and the evil (3-5, 7-8). Some issues mentioned here are devotion, integrity, discernment and commitment. Our outlook determines our outcome.

102 Depression (102:11)   □✱□✱□

This psalm may be a conversation of Jesus on the cross with his Father, the Father's answer, the comments of the Holy Spirit, and a conclusion by Jesus. This psalm also presents a prayer (1-2), some ten symptoms of depression (3-11), nine helps for the depressed (12-22), and six characteristic of the change that comes with depression (23-28). In God there is healing for spiritual depression. Sometimes healing takes time, at other instances it is quite fast.

103 Bless the Lord (103:12) ☐✸☐✸☐

As His children, we bless the Lord with gratitude. He blesses us in at least six ways (1-5, 8-13). What more can we want? He knows that we are but dust or grass (14-16).

1 Bless the LORD, O my soul: and all that is within me, bless his holy name.

2 Bless the LORD, O my soul, and forget not all his benefits, such as _____.

3 Who forgives all your iniquities; who heals all your diseases;

4 Who redeems your life from destruction; who crowns you with loving kindness and tender mercies;

5 Who satisfies your mouth with good things; so that your youth is renewed like the eagle's and you can still _____.

6 The LORD executes righteousness and judgment for all that are oppressed.

7 He made known his ways unto Moses, his acts to the children of Israel.

8The LORD is merciful and gracious, slow to anger, and plenteous in mercy.

9 He will not always chide: neither will he keep his anger forever.

10 He has not dealt with us after our sins; nor rewarded us according to our iniquities.

11 For as the heaven is high above the earth, so great is his mercy toward them that fear him.

12 As far as the east is from the west, so far has he removed our transgressions from us.

13 Like as a father pities his children, so the LORD pities them that fear him.

14 For he knows our frame; he remembers that we are dust.

15 As for man, his days are as grass: as a flower of the field, so he flourishes.

16 For the wind passes over it, and it is gone; and the place thereof shall know it no more.

17 But the mercy of the LORD is from everlasting to everlasting upon them that fear him, and his righteousness unto children's children;

18 To such as keep his covenant, and to those that remember his commandments to do them. **19** The LORD hath prepared his throne in the heavens; and his kingdom rules over all.

20 Bless the LORD, you his angels, that excel in strength, that do his commandments, hearkening unto the voice of his word. **21** Bless the LORD, all you his hosts; you ministers of his, that do his pleasure.

22 Bless the LORD, all his works in all places of his dominion: bless the LORD, O my soul.

104 Managing His Creation (104:24) □✱□✱□

God manages well what he created in seven days. This psalm is similar to Genesis 1. The Lord made and provides for us water, food, plants, trees, homes, and time (10-23, 25-30). Praise the Creator.

105 Out of Egypt (105:11) ☐✱☐✱☐

This is the covenant God made with Abraham. All depends on God. Keep searching for God (1-5). The psalm traces God's guidance in the time of Abraham, Joseph, Moses and Joshua (6-45). In verses 26-36 it lists the ten plagues that rained on Egypt.

1 O give thanks to the LORD; call on his name: make known his deeds among the people.

2 Sing to him, sing psalms to him: talk of all his wondrous works like

_____.

3 Glory in his holy name: let the heart of them rejoice that seek the LORD.

4 Seek the LORD, and his strength: seek his face evermore.

5 Remember his marvelous works that he has done; his wonders, and the judgments of his mouth;

6 O you seed of Abraham his servant, you children of Jacob his chosen.

7 He is the LORD our God: his judgments are in all the earth.

8 He has remembered his covenant forever, the word which he commanded to a thousand generations.

9 Which covenant he made with Abraham, and his oath to Isaac;

10 And confirmed the same to Jacob for a law, and to Israel for an everlasting covenant:

11 Saying, Unto you will I give the land of Canaan, the lot of your inheritance:

12 When they were but a few men in number; indeed very few, and strangers in it.

13 When they went from one nation to another, from one kingdom to another people;

14 He suffered no man to do them wrong: yes, he reproved kings for their sakes;

15 Saying, Touch not my anointed, and do my prophets no harm.

16 Moreover he called for a famine upon the land: he broke the whole staff of bread.

17 He sent a man before them, even Joseph, who was sold for a servant:

18 Whose feet they hurt with fetters: he was laid in iron:

19 Until the time that his word came: the word of the LORD tried him.

20 The king sent and loosed him; even the ruler of the people, and let him go free.

21 He made him lord of his house, and ruler of all his substance:

22 To bind his princes at his pleasure; and teach his senators wisdom.

23 Israel also came into Egypt; and Jacob sojourned in the land of Ham.

24 And he increased his people greatly; and made them stronger than their enemies.

25 He turned their heart to hate his people, to deal subtly with his servants.

26 He sent Moses his servant; and Aaron whom he had chosen.

27 They showed his signs among them, and wonders in the land of Ham.

28 He sent darkness, and made it dark; and they rebelled not against his word.

29 He turned their waters into blood, and slew their fish.

30 Their land brought forth frogs in abundance, in the chambers of their kings.

31 He spoke, and there came divers sorts of flies, and lice in all their coasts.

32 He gave them hail for rain, and flaming fire in their land.

33 He smote their vines also and their fig trees; and broke the trees of their coasts.

34 He spoke, and the locusts came, and caterpillars and that without number,

35 And did eat up all the herbs in their land, and devoured the fruit of their ground.

36 He smote also all the firstborn in their land, the chief of all their strength.

37 He brought them forth also with silver and gold: and there was not one feeble person among their tribes.

38 Egypt was glad when they departed: for the fear of them fell upon them.

39 He spread a cloud for a covering; and fire to give light in the night.

40 The people asked, and he brought quails, and satisfied them with the bread of heaven.

41 He opened the rock, and the waters gushed out; they ran in the dry places like a river.

42 For he remembered his holy promise, and Abraham his servant.

43 And he brought forth his people with joy, and his chosen with gladness: We too escaped _____.

44 And gave them the lands of the heathen: and they inherited the labor of the people;

45 That they might observe his statutes, and keep his laws. Praise the LORD.

106 Failures and Hope (106:8) ☐✱☐✱☐

The writer of this psalm asks God to regard Israel, to redeem Israel and to gather back the people of Israel (1-5, 48). This psalm further deals with the past ten sins of Israel (6-46) and God's six acts of compassion (8-12, 43-46). History unfolds the acts of God's people and of God.

Book Five, Singer: Psalm 107-150

107 Help in Distress (107:6) ☐✱☐✱☐

We live with stress. But here are rescue, recovery and deliverance. In verses 4-9, some lose their way, in verses 10-16 their freedom, in verses 17-22 their health, in verses 23-32 their hope. Nevertheless, give thanks. God gathers, He feeds, He leads, He heals, He saves.

1 O give thanks to the LORD, for he is good: for his mercy endures forever.

2 Let the redeemed of the LORD say so, whom he has redeemed from the hand of the enemy;

3 And gathered them out of the lands, from the east, and from the west, from the north, and from the south.

4 They wandered in the wilderness in a solitary way; they found no city to dwell in.

5 Hungry and thirsty, their soul fainted in them.

6 Then they cried unto the LORD in their trouble, and he delivered them out of their distresses.

7 And he led them forth by the right way, that they might go to a city of habitation.

8 Oh that men would praise the LORD for his goodness, and for his wonderful works to the children of men!

9 For he satisfies the longing soul, and fills the hungry soul with goodness.

10 Such as sit in darkness and in the shadow of death, being bound in affliction and iron;

11 Because they rebelled against the words of God, and contemned the counsel of the most High:

12 Therefore he brought down their heart with labor; they fell down, and there was none to help.

13 Then they cried unto the LORD in their trouble, and he saved them out of their distresses.

14 He brought them out of darkness and the shadow of death, and broke their bands in sunder.

15 Oh that men would praise the LORD for his goodness, and for his wonderful works to the children of men!

16 For he hath broken the gates of brass, and cut the bars of iron in sunder.

17 Fools because of their transgression, and because of their iniquities, are afflicted.

18 Their soul arbores all manner of meat; and they draw near unto the gates of death.

19 Then they cry to the LORD in their trouble, and he saves them out of their distresses.

20 He sent his word, and healed them, and delivered them from their destructions.

21 Oh that men would praise the LORD for his goodness, and for his wonderful works to the children of men!

22 And let them sacrifice the sacrifices of thanksgiving, and declare his works with rejoicing.

23 They that go down to the sea in ships, that do business in great waters;

24 These see the works of the LORD, and his wonders in the deep.

25 For he commands, and raises the stormy wind, which lifts up the waves thereof.

26 They mount up to the heaven, they go down again to the depths: their soul is melted because of trouble.

27 They reel to and fro, and stagger like a drunken man, and are at their wit's end.

28 Then they cry to the LORD in their trouble, and he brings them out of their distresses by _____.

29 He makes the storm calm, so that the waves thereof are still.

30 Then are they glad because they are quiet; so he brings them unto their desired haven.

31 Oh that men would praise the LORD for his goodness, and for his wonderful works to the children of men!

32 Let them exalt him also in the congregation of the people, and praise him in the assembly of the elders.

33 He turns rivers into a wilderness, and the water springs into dry ground;

34 A fruitful land into barrenness, for the wickedness of them that dwell therein.

35 He turns the wilderness into a standing water, and dry ground into water springs by _____.

36 And there he makes the hungry to dwell, that they may prepare a city for habitation;

37 And sow the fields, and plant vineyards, which may yield fruits of increase.

38 He blesses them also, so that they are multiplied greatly; and he does not let their cattle decrease.

39 Again, they are diminished and brought low through oppression, affliction, and sorrow.

40 He pours contempt upon princes, and causes them to wander in the wilderness, where there is no way.

41 Yet sets he the poor on high from affliction, and makes him families like a flock.

42 The righteous shall see it, and rejoice: and all iniquity shall stop her mouth.

43 Whoso is wise, and will observe these things, even they shall understand the loving kindness of the LORD.

108 Praise the Lord (108:12)   □✱□✱□

*The first five verses are like Psalm 57:7-11 and others like 60:5-12.
Praise God again. Verses 9-12 seem to refer to Petra. The psalm is
full of praise to the Lord. David here answers some basic questions
about worship: how, when, where, and why (1-5, 7-10.) He asks for
God's help (11-13).*

109 It's Time for Judgment (109:26)   □✱□✱□

*This Psalm curses God's enemies and records their punishment.
Lord, please judge Saul and the wicked; Lord please help. Notice the
5 "but's" in verses 4, 16, 21, and 28.*

110 Priest and King (110:1)   □✱□✱□

*Christ will return to earth. He is God (1), He is king (2-3), He is priest
(4), He is judge (6), He is a warrior (5-7). Christ is priest after the
order of Melchizedek (4).*

111 The Works of the Lord (111:10)   □✱□✱□

*The Lord is great (1-2.) This psalm is an acrostic about the works of
God (2-4, 6, 7). It tells us where wisdom starts and how the law fits
in (10).*

9 He sent redemption unto his people: he has commanded his
covenant for ever: holy and reverend is his name. **10 The fear of
the LORD is the beginning of wisdom: a good understanding
have all they that do his commandments: his praise endures
forever.**

112 Blessed (112:7) ☐✷☐✷☐

An acrostic continuation of Psalm 111. It praises the uprightness of the faithful. It deals with the love of the God's word, with love and compassion, with giving. The faithful are blessed in many ways.

113 Hallelujah, Praise the Lord (113:7) ☐✷☐✷☐

This psalm is a hallel (praise song) about the Lord. Actually many psalms are praise songs, but this one is especially designated as one. God has horizontal glory (1-3) and vertical glory (4-6). He has mercy (7-9).

114 The Exodus (114:7) ☐✷☐✷☐

God did great things for Israel. Two of these great miracles were the Exodus from Egypt (1-3) and the crossing of the Jordan (3-8).

115 Dead Idols (115:3) ☐✷☐✷☐

We resemble our idols. We become like them (8). The Lord is faithful (1-3). Notice the seven nonfunctioning parts of an idol (4-7). He will bless the faithful and the faithful will bless Him (12-18).

116 Deliver Us (116:15) ☐✱☐✱☐

The Lord is risen and we sing Him our thanks for our deliverance (1-11). This is a very personal psalm with the words "I, my, me" used some 30 times. Death is an appointment, not an accident (15).

15 Precious in the sight of the LORD is the death of his saints.

16 O LORD, truly I am your servant; I am your servant, and the son of your handmaid: you have loosed my bonds.

17 I will offer to you the sacrifice of thanksgiving, and will call upon the name of the LORD.

117. The King of the Gentiles (117:1) ☐✱☐✱☐

God's people are separate but not isolated. We live by faith and are saved by grace. This is the shortest psalm and chapter in the Bible.

118 Christ Returns (118:22) ☐✱☐✱☐

A praise song about God's enduing love sung after the Passover meal. It is the last of the Hallels (praise songs). His mercy endures.

119 Aleph: Obey the Word (7)   ☐✱☐✱☐

*This psalm is an acrostic in 22 parts about the value of the Bible.
Each of the 22 sections of the psalm consists of eight verses and is
here presented as a separate prayer. This Psalm starts with Alphi
and ends with Tau, the first and last letters of the Hebrew alphabet.
Each line in the first section starts in Hebrew with Alphi, in the
second section with Beth, and so on. With 176 verses, it is the
longest chapter in the Bible. Each verse includes the word "precepts"
or one of its synonyms. List and count your blessings. They are so
plentiful. We show our appreciation for them by obeying God's Word.*

1 Blessed are the undefiled in the way, who walk in the law of the
LORD.

2 Blessed are they that keep his testimonies, and that seek him with
the whole heart by _____.

3 They also do no iniquity: they walk in his ways.

4 You have commanded us to keep your precepts diligently.

5 O that my ways were directed to keep your statutes!

6 Then shall I not be ashamed, when I have respect unto all your
commandments.

**7 I will praise you with uprightness of heart, when I shall have
learned your righteous judgments.**

8 I will keep your statutes: O forsake me not utterly.

119 Beth: Cleaned by the Word (11)   □✱□✱□

While the word "Bible" is not used in the Bible or in the Psalms, eight words that have a similar meaning are: law, testimony, precept, statue, commandment, judgment, word, and promise. As we study our Bibles, God's Word cleanses our lives. Thus we keep pure.

9 Wherewithal shall a young man cleanse his way? by taking heed thereto according to your word and _____.

 10 With my whole heart have I sought you: O let me not wander from your commandments.

 11 Your word have I hid in my heart, that I might not sin against you.

 12 Blessed are you, O LORD: teach me your statutes.

 13 With my lips have I declared all the judgments of your mouth.

 14 I have rejoiced in the way of your testimonies, as much as in all riches.

 15 I will meditate on your precepts, and have respect to your ways.

 16 I will delight myself in your statutes: I will not forget your word.

119 Gimel: Need of the Word (18) □✱□✱□

We need God and His Word. Without them, we can do nothing. In order to appreciate the Bible, we need our eyes opened. We study it, memorize it, enjoy it. Note the similarity between Psalms 119 and Psalm 19.

17 Deal bountifully with your servant, that I may live, and keep your word.

18 Open my eyes, that I may behold wondrous things out of your law, such as _____.

19 I am a stranger in the earth: hide not your commandments from me.

20 My soul breaks for the longing that it has to your judgments at all times.

21 You have rebuked the proud that are cursed, which do err from your commandments.

22 Remove from me reproach and contempt; for I have kept your testimonies.

23 Princes also did sit and speak against me: but your servant did meditate in your statutes.

24 Your testimonies also are my delight and my counselors.

119 Daleth: Revived by the Word (27) □*□*□

The Word of God has restoring and reviving power. It does that by teaching us, strengthening us, defending us. We need to understand the way of God's precepts.

25 My soul cleaves unto the dust: quicken me according to your word.

26 I have declared my ways, and you heard me: teach me your statutes by _____.

27 Make me to understand the way of your precepts: so shall I talk of your wondrous works.

28 My soul melts for heaviness: strengthen me according to your word.

29 Remove from me the way of lying: and grant me your law graciously.

30 I have chosen the way of truth: your judgments have I laid before me.

31 I have stuck to your testimonies: O LORD, put me not to shame.

32 I will run the way of your commandments, when you shall enlarge my heart.

119 He: Empowered by the Word (37)   □*□*□

God is willing to help us turn precepts into powerful practice. Our outlook determines the outcome. Here the first four verses lean toward the positive, the last four toward the negative.

33 Teach me, O LORD, the way of your statutes; and I shall keep it unto the end.

34 Give me understanding, and I shall keep your law; yes, I shall observe it with my whole heart.

35 Make me to go in the path of your commandments; for therein do I delight.

36 Incline my heart unto your testimonies, and not to covetousness.

37 Turn away my eyes from beholding vanity; and quicken me in your way in _____.

38 Establish your word to your servant, who is devoted to your fear.

39 Turn away my reproach which I fear: for your judgments are good.

40 Behold, I have longed after your precepts: quicken me in your righteousness.

119 Waw: Victorious by the Word (45) ☐✱☐✱☐

There is no other way to the victorious life except by the Word. Notice the five things the believer will do as listed in verses 45-48. We go from faith to hope to love, from the past, into the present and into the future.

 41 Let your mercies come also unto me, O LORD, even your salvation, according to your word.

 42 So shall I have wherewith to answer him that reproaches me: for I trust in your word.

 43 And take not the word of truth utterly out of my mouth; for I have hoped in your judgments.

 44 So shall I keep your law continually forever and ever.

 **45 And I will walk at liberty: (how?) _____
for I seek your precepts.**

 46 I will speak of your testimonies also before kings, and will not be ashamed.

 47 And I will delight myself in your commandments, which I have loved.

 48 My hands also will I lift up unto your commandments, which I have loved; and I will meditate in your statutes.

119 Zayin: Rest in the Word (54) ☐✽☐✽☐

Here the psalmist reminds God to remember him. Then he tells God twice that he remembers Him. He sings God's statutes in the house of his pilgrimage. The law has become his law.

49 Remember the word to your servant, upon which you have caused me to hope.

50 This is my comfort in my affliction: for your word has quickened me.

51 The proud have had me greatly in derision: yet have I not declined from your law.

52 I remembered your judgments of old, O LORD; and have comforted myself.

53 Horror has taken hold upon me because of the wicked that forsake your law.

54 Your statutes have been my songs in the house of my pilgrimage in that _____.

55 I have remembered your name, O LORD, in the night, and have kept your law.

56 This I had, because I kept your precepts.

119 Heth: Preserved by the Word (59) □✱□✱□

God meets our needs. The psalmist here thought about his way and his feet and made haste to keep God's commandments. Here is a companion of all who fear God.

57 You are my portion, O LORD: I have said that I would keep your words.

58 I entreated your favor with my whole heart: be merciful unto me according to your word.

59 I thought on my ways, and turned my feet to your testimonies by _____.

60 I made haste, and delayed not to keep your commandments.

61 The bands of the wicked have robbed me: but I have not forgotten your law.

62 At midnight I will rise to give thanks unto you because of your righteous judgments.

63 I am a companion of all them that fear you, and of them that keep your precepts.

64 The earth, O LORD, is full of your mercy: teach me your statutes.

119 Teth: The Goodness of the Word (66)   □✱□✱□

The psalmist here asks the Lord to teach him good judgment, knowledge, and his statues. He learned through affliction. In verse 71 it gives the reason for his affliction.

65 You have dealt well with your servant, O LORD, according unto your word.

66 Teach me good judgment and knowledge: for I have believed your commandments.

67 Before I was afflicted I went astray: but now have I kept your word.

68 You are good, and do good; teach me your statutes.

69 The proud have forged a lie against me: but I will keep your precepts with my whole heart.

70 Their heart is as fat as grease; but I delight in your law.

71 It is good for me that I have been afflicted in _____; that I might learn your statutes.

72 The law of your mouth is better unto me than mountains of gold and silver.

119 Yod: Insights by the Word (73) □✱□✱□

The Creator has written an instruction book for His creatures. Read the instructions. And again the psalmist writes about his afflictions. He asks God to comfort him, to make God's law his delight.

73 Your hands have made me and fashioned me: give me understanding, that I may learn your commandments.

74 They that fear you will be glad when they see me; because I have hoped in your word.

75 I know, O LORD, that your judgments are right, and that you in faithfulness have afflicted me.

76 Let, I pray, your merciful kindness be for my comfort, according to your word unto your servant and _____.

77 Let your tender mercies come to me, that I may live: for your law is my delight.

78 Let the proud be ashamed; for they dealt perversely with me without a cause: but I will meditate on your precepts.

79 Let those that fear you turn to me, and those that have known your testimonies.

80 Let my heart be sound in your statutes; that I be not ashamed.

119 Kath: Sustained by the Word (88)   □*□*□

In this psalm the emphasis is on hope, time and patience. His two big questions here are about the time of God's judgment. He needs God's help to survive.

81 My soul faints for your salvation: but I hope in your word.

82 My eyes fail for your word, saying, When will you comfort me?_____

83 For I am become like a bottle in the smoke; yet do I not forget your statutes.

84 How many are the days of your servant? when will you execute judgment on them that persecute me?

85 The proud have dug pits for me, which are not after your law.

86 All your commandments are faithful: they persecute me wrongfully; help me.

87 They had almost consumed me upon earth; but I forsook not your precepts.

88 Quicken me after your loving kindness; so shall I keep the testimony of your mouth.

119 Lamed: Changelessness of the Word (92) □✱□✱□

In a world of change, God is changeless. Nothing is perfect, except God and his law. In five statements, the psalmist assures us of the permanency of God's Word.

89 Forever, O LORD, your word is settled in heaven.

90 Your faithfulness is unto all generations: you have established the earth, and it abides.

91 They continue this day according to your ordinances: for all are your servants.

92 Unless your law had been my delight, I should then have perished in mine affliction and _____.

93 I will never forget your precepts: for with them you have quickened me.

94 I am yours, save me: for I have sought your precepts.

95 The wicked have waited for me to destroy me: but I will consider your testimonies.

96 I have seen an end of all perfection: but your commandment is exceeding broad.

119 Mem: Receive Wisdom by the Word (99)   □✶□✶□

The psalmist here states that he is wiser with more understanding than three groups of people. He gives God the credit for that. The Word of God is sweeter than honey.

97 O how I love your law! it is my meditation all the day.

98 You through your commandments have made me wiser than mine enemies: for they are ever with me.

99 I have more understanding than all my teachers: for your testimonies are my meditation.

100 I understand more than the ancients, because I keep your precepts.

101 I have refrained my feet from every evil way, that I might keep your word.

102 I have not departed from your judgments: for you have taught me.

103 How sweet are your words to my taste! yes, sweeter than honey to my mouth! They taste _____.

104 Through your precepts I get understanding: therefore I hate every false way.

119 Nun: Enlightened by the Word (105) □✱□✱□

The psalmist walks one step at the time in the Light of the Lord. He trusts God and sees far enough what is ahead. He again talks about his affliction and asks God to revive him, accept him and teach him.

105 Your word is a lamp to my feet, and a light to my path.

106 I have sworn, and I will perform it, that I will keep your righteous judgments.

107 I am afflicted very much: quicken me, O LORD, according to your word.

108 Accept, I beseech you, the freewill offerings of my mouth, which are

_____

LORD, and teach me your judgments.

109 My soul is continually in my hand: yet do I not forget your law.

110 The wicked have laid a snare for me: yet I erred not from your precepts.

111 Your testimonies have I taken as a heritage for ever: for they are the rejoicing of my heart.

112 I have inclined my heart to perform your statutes always, even unto the end.

119 Samek: The Enemy of the Word (114) □✶□✶□

The double-minded are half-hearted. The whole psalm is a contrast between good and evil. Good wins, evil fails. The psalmist fears (in a positive way) and respects God's judgments (120).

113 I hate the double-minded: _____ but your law do I love.

114 You are my hiding place and my shield: I hope in your word.

115 Depart from me, ye evildoers: for I will keep the commandments of my God.

116 Uphold me according unto your word, that I may live: and let me not be ashamed of my hope.

117 Hold me up, and I shall be safe: and I will have respect to your statutes continually.

118 You have trodden down all them that err from your statutes: for their deceit is falsehood.

119 You put away all the wicked of the earth like dross: therefore I love your testimonies.

120 My flesh trembles for fear of you; and I am afraid of your judgments.

119 Ayin: Delivered by the Word (128)   ☐✷☐✷☐

The psalmist tries to get away from the oppressor. He asks for mercy and to be given understanding. There is a right way out. The psalmist hates every evil way.

121 I have done judgment and justice: leave me not to my oppressors.

122 Be surety for your servant for good: let not the proud oppress me.

123 My eyes fail for your salvation, and for the word of your righteousness.

124 Deal with your servant according unto your mercy, and teach me your statutes.

125 I am your servant; give me understanding, that I may know your testimonies and _____.

126 It is time for you, LORD, to work: for they have made void your law.

127 Therefore I love your commandments above gold; yea, above fine gold.

128 Therefore I esteem all your precepts concerning all things to be right; and I hate every false way.

119 Pe: The Word Gives Light (130) □✱□✱□

The psalmist, on the one hand, learns from the law, on the other hand, laments those who do not keep the law. He asks that God would direct his steps by His Word.

129 Your testimonies are wonderful: therefore my soul keep them.

130 The entrance of your words gives light; it gives understanding unto the simple.

131 I opened my mouth, and panted: for I longed for your commandments in that I _____.

132 Look upon me, and be merciful unto me, as you used to do unto those that love your name.

133 Order my steps in your word: and let not any iniquity have dominion over me.

134 Deliver me from the oppression of man: so will I keep your precepts.

135 Make your face to shine upon your servant; and teach me your statutes.

136 Rivers of waters run down mine eyes, because they keep not your law.

119 Tsadde: Be Zealous for the Word (139) ☐✱☐✱☐

That is where all the true righteousness resides. In contrast to God, the psalmist considers himself small.

137 Righteous are you, O LORD, and upright are your judgments.

138 Your testimonies that you have commanded are righteous and very faithful.

139 My zeal hath consumed me,

---

because my enemies have forgotten your words.

140 Your word is very pure: therefore your servant loves it.

141 I am small and despised: yet do not I forget your precepts.

142 Your righteousness is an everlasting righteousness, and your law is the truth.

143 Trouble and anguish have taken hold on me: yet your commandments are my delights.

144 The righteousness of your testimonies is everlasting: give me understanding, and I shall live.

119 Qoph: Experience the Word (149)   □✱□✱□

Verses 145-149 are a very personal primer on prayer. Here the pronoun "I" or "me" is used eight times. The psalm presents an attitude of prayer. The psalmist is indeed a man of prayer.

145 I cried with my whole heart; hear me, O LORD: I will keep your statutes.

146 I cried unto you; save me, and I shall keep your testimonies.

147 I prevented the dawning of the morning, and cried: I hoped in your word.

148 My eyes prevent the night watches, that I might meditate on your word.

149 Hear my voice according to your loving kindness: O LORD, quicken me according to your judgment.

150 They draw nigh that follow after mischief: they are far from your law.

151 You are near, O LORD; and all your commandments are truth. I know that because _____.

152 Concerning your testimonies, I have known of old that you have founded them forever.

119 Resh: Strengthened by the Word (159)   □✱□✱□

This is a prayer for a personal revival. The word "revive" is used three times. God's Word is one of the agents of revival. God hears. God's Word is truth.

153 Consider my affliction, and deliver me: for I do not forget your law.

154 Plead my cause, and deliver me: revive me according to your word.

155 Salvation is far from the wicked: for they seek not your statutes.

156 Great are your tender mercies, O LORD: revive me according to your judgments and _____.

157 Many are my persecutors and my enemies; yet do I not decline from your testimonies.

158 I beheld the transgressors, and was grieved; because they kept not your word.

159 Consider how I love your precepts: revive me, O LORD, according to your loving kindness.

160 Your word is true from the beginning: and every one of your righteous judgments endures forever.

119 Shin: Perfected by the Word (165) ☐✱☐✱☐

The psalmist keeps praising God all day. He writes that he praises God seven times a day. That may be at rising, at breakfast, at work, at noon, in the afternoon, at supper and at bed time. Praise of God brings peace. There is healing of many wrongs in the word of God.

161 Princes have persecuted me without a cause: but my heart stands in awe of your word.

162 I rejoice at your word, as one that finds great spoil.

163 I hate and abhor lying: but your law do I love.

164 Seven times a day do I praise you because of your righteous judgments. When?_____

165 Great peace have they which love your law: and nothing shall offend them.

166 LORD, I have hoped for your salvation, and done your commandments.

167 My soul hath kept your testimonies; and I love them exceedingly.

168 I have kept your precepts and your testimonies: for all my ways are before you.

119 Tau: Helped by the Word (176)   □✱□✱□

This is the last part of Psalm 119. This is a plea for help. It talks about my cry, my supplication, my lips, my tongue and my soul. After all this, the psalmist knows that he is like a lost sheep in need of being looked after.

169 Let my cry come near before you, O LORD: give me understanding according to your word.

170 Let my supplication come before you: deliver me according to your word.

171 My lips shall utter praise, when you hast taught me your statutes.

172 My tongue shall speak of your word: for all your commandments are righteousness.

173 Let your hand help me; for I have chosen your precepts.

174 I have longed for your salvation, O LORD; and your law is my delight.

175 Let my soul live, and it shall praise you; and let your judgments help me in _____.

176 I have gone astray like a lost sheep; seek your servant; for I do not forget your commandments.

Psalm 120-134: Pilgrim Psalms

Psalms 120-134 are called the Pilgrim Psalms and consist of the songs the Israelites sang as they went up three times a year to the temple. There are 14 of these Psalms of Ascents.

120 The Distressed (120:1)   ☐✸☐✸☐

When troubled and stressed, we have a God who hears us. That is a blessing. We are never alone in our troubles. The psalmist prays to be saved from the evil tongue and the warring people. Some in this world hate peace and others are for peace.

121 The Lord as Keeper (121:5) ☐✱☐✱☐

This Psalm is the second Song of Ascent and one of the most beautiful. I look up to God (1-2). The Holy Spirit guarantees our safety. God is the creator, our constant helper, our protector, our life preserver day and night (3-8).

1 I will lift up mine eyes unto the hills. From where comes my help?

2 My help cometh from the LORD, who made heaven and earth.

3 He will not suffer your foot to be moved: he that keeps you will not slumber.

4 Behold, he who keeps Israel shall neither slumber nor sleep.

**5 The LORD is your keeper in _____:
the LORD is your shade upon your right hand.**

6 The sun shall not smite you by day, nor the moon by night.

7 The LORD shall preserve you from all evil: he shall preserve your soul.

8 The LORD shall preserve your going out and your coming in from this time forth, and even for evermore.

122 In the Lord's Presence (122:1) ☐✱☐✱☐

It is a great joy to worship the Lord wherever we are. This psalm centers on worship in Jerusalem. It includes both praise for Jerusalem (1-5) and a prayer for Jerusalem for peace, protection and prosperity (6-9).

1 I was glad when they said unto me, Let us go into the house of the LORD because _____.

2 Our feet shall stand within your gates, O Jerusalem.

3 Jerusalem is built as a city that is compact together:

123 Look Toward God (123:2) ☐✱☐✱☐

As escapees in Babylon, God's people looked for God's mercy. The word "eyes" is used four times in the first two verses. Described here is a servant-master relationship of a maid and her mistress (1-2) and a persecutor-protector relationship (3-4)

124 The Great Escape (124:7)   ☐✸☐✸☐

The Jews and we were trapped many times. They and we are here to thank the Lord for his help in our escapes. We got away, we got a way out in Jesus. Verses 3-7 tells how Noah got away when the flood came, how Daniel got away from the lions, and how David got away from Goliath and Saul. Our help is in God. Noah, Rahab, Lot and Paul all got away. God provides the clues that help us escape. We have here the worst (1-5) and the best (6-8) of all worlds.

1 If it had not been for the LORD who was on our side, now may Israel say:

2 If it had not been for the LORD who was on our side, when men rose up against us:

3 Then they had swallowed us up quickly, when their wrath was kindled against us:

4 Then the waters had overwhelmed us, the stream had gone over our soul:

5 Then the proud waters had gone over our soul.

6 Blessed be the LORD, who hath not given us as a prey to their teeth.

7 Our soul is escaped as a bird out of the snare of the fowlers: the snare is broken, and we are escaped to _____.

8 Our help is in the name of the LORD, who made heaven and earth for he _____.

125 God Protects His People (125:2) ☐✱☐✱☐

This psalm was written in the time of Nehemiah. It describes those who trust the Lord. Nothing can harm us except by God's permission. God delivers (1-3) and hears our requests (4-5).

126 Sow and Reap (126:6) ☐✱☐✱☐

The captives return from Persia. King Cyrus has freed the Jews. They rejoice in their new freedom. The first year of their return was rather hard. With difficulty we spread the Word of God and with joy we will see the results of it. Those who expect to reap must first sow

127 Children as Blessings (127:3) ☐✱☐✱☐

Here we have four illustrations that all things without God are worthless: house construction, security guards, long work-hours and family building (1-2). Solomon here talks of the blessings children can bring (3-5).

3 Lo, children are a heritage of the LORD: and the fruit of the womb is his reward even when _____.

4 As arrows are in the hand of a mighty man; so are children of the youth.

5 Happy is the man that hath his quiver full of them: they shall not be ashamed, but they shall speak with the enemies in the gate.

128 Kinds of Blessings (128:6)　☐✶☐✶☐

As followers of God, we receive blessings of longevity, happiness, prosperity and productivity (1-2). The psalm also talks about the blessings of a wife, children and grandchildren (3-6).

129 The Afflicted Survive (129:2)　☐✶☐✶☐

During most of its days, Israel has been afflicted. Often their extinction was close, but they have survived until this day. Sometimes suffering is the lot of the faithful. But in God's hands, we too survive. We are blessed anyway.

130 Forgiveness (130:7)　☐✶☐✶☐

We often pray when we have no one else to turn to. We can receive both the forgiveness from God and the mercy of God. Our hope is in God. Here the psalmist first talks about this to God (1-6) and then to Israel (7-8).

131 Accept Yourself (131:1)　☐✶☐✶☐

There are mysteries that can't be explained here. We can accept God and ourselves without ever learning some of the circumstances that affect us. David does not have all the answers that life throws at mankind. But we can hope in the Lord.

132 Dedication of the Temple (132:13) □*□*□

 The ark comes to Jerusalem. It looks as if we find here Solomon's prayer that God's Shekinah glory would dwell above the ark. God answered Solomon. David wanted to build a house for God   (1-10) and was told by God that He will establish the house of David (11-18).

133 Unity (133:1) □*□*□

David talks about his joy in worshiping God and fellowshipping with other believers. This short psalm promises pleasantness, refreshment and God's blessing. The ointment mentioned here may be a study in itself.

134 Blessing and Benediction (134:2) □*□*□

The last of the 14 Pilgrim Psalms calls for us two times to bless the Lord. In turn, the Lord blesses us in connection with our worship. The night watchman of the temple lifts up his hands in blessing. Worship never ends.

135 Reasons for Praising God (135:6) □*□*□

There are at least seven reasons to praise God. And personally, we have many more. We can make our own lists. In this psalm, many reasons start with the word "for" or "who". There is a great difference between the true God (1-14, 9-12) and false gods (25-18).

136 The Great Hellel (136:1) ☐✱☐✱☐

Sung at the Passover, New Year and many other occasions, each verse has an antiphonal identical response: " his mercy endures forever". Thanks. The word "Hallel" comes from the Hebrew hallelujah, which means praise the Lord. The psalm lists many reasons to thank the Lord. It starts with a call to worship (1-3), then thanks to our Creator (4-9), Redeemer (10-15), Guide (16), Champion (17-22) Helper, Savior, Provider (23-25) and the God of heaven (26).

1 O give thanks unto the LORD; for he is good: for his mercy endures forever and he _____.

2 O give thanks unto the God of gods: for his mercy endures forever.

3 O give thanks to the Lord of lords: for his mercy endures forever.

4 To him who alone does great wonders: for his mercy endures forever.

5 To him that by wisdom made the heavens: for his mercy endures forever.

6 To him that stretched out the earth above the waters: for his mercy endures forever.

7 To him that made great lights: for his mercy endures forever:

8 The sun to rule by day: for his mercy endures forever:

9 The moon and stars to rule by night: for his mercy endures forever.

10 To him that smote Egypt in their firstborn: for his mercy endures forever:

11 And brought out Israel from among them: for his mercy endures forever:

12 With a strong hand, and with a stretched out arm: for his mercy endures forever.

13 To him which divided the Red Sea into parts: for his mercy endures forever:

14 And made Israel to pass through the midst of it: for his mercy endures forever:

15 But overthrew Pharaoh and his host in the Red Sea: for his mercy endures forever.

16 To him which led his people through the wilderness: for his mercy endures forever.

17 To him which smote great kings: for his mercy endures forever:

18 And slew famous kings: for his mercy endures forever:

19 Sihon king of the Amorites: for his mercy endures forever:

20 And Og the king of Bashan: for his mercy endures forever:

21 And gave their land for a heritage: for his mercy endures forever:

22 Even a heritage unto Israel his servant: for his mercy endures forever.

23 Who remembered us in our low estate: for his mercy endures forever:

24 And has redeemed us from our enemies: for his mercy endures forever.

25 Who gives food to all flesh: for his mercy endures forever.

26 O give thanks unto the God of heaven: for his mercy endures forever and

_____.

137 Don't Forget Jerusalem (137:4)   ☐✱☐✱☐

After the captivity, the Jews remembered how they had gathered on the Sabbaths by the rivers of Babylon to pray. There they could not sing the happy songs of Zion. To the Hebrews, singing was more than music, it was a deep expression of the heart. The words "O Jerusalem" have become the rallying cry of the Jews down through the ages. Verses 7-9 are history that has been prophesied in Isaiah 13:16. The verses may have a spiritual application in that little sins must be destroyed or they will destroy us.

3 For there they that carried us away captive required of us a song; and they that wasted us required of us mirth, saying, sing us one of the songs of Zion.

4 How shall we sing the LORD's song in a strange land?

_____.

5 If I forget you, O Jerusalem, let my right hand forget her cunning.

138 In Trouble (138:7)   ☐✱☐✱☐

David thanks God for saving him in trouble. We do the same. David had many great answers to prayer, and so do we, if we can just see the hand of God working for us. He encourages us, strengthens us, preserves us, and guides us (3, 7-8). We can be bold with strength in our souls (3).

139 God is Everywhere (139:7) ☐✱☐✱☐

There is nothing God does not know, where he is not, and what he cannot do. God is great. We cannot escape his presence. The psalm describes God's omniscience (1-6). His omnipresence (7-12), and His omnipotence (13-24). We are very foolish when we try to run away from God. We cannot deceive Him, escape Him or ignore Him.

140 Prayer for Deliverance (140:1) ☐✱☐✱☐

David draws near to God for protection and deliverance from Saul's men. David contrasts what the godless do and deserve (1-11) and the blessings of the godly (12-13).

141 Making Wise Decisions (141:2) ☐✱☐✱☐

The young David asks the Lord for help, for wise words and a way of escape. He asks God to hear his prayer (1-2) and to honor the specifics of it (3-10). David makes a strange request for the righteous to reprove him in the Lord (5). He does not refuse their reproof (5).

142 Forsaken (142:7) ☐✱☐✱☐

David is pursued by enemies, deserted by friends, and hiding in a cave. Forsaken by men and alone, he does not feel forsaken by God. That is faith. David is desperate (1-4), but hopeful in the Lord, his Rescuer (5-7).

143 Twelve Aspects of Prayer (143:10) □*□*□

Each of the twelve verses of this Psalm deals with a different aspect of prayer. Each verse is a plea for something specific. Whatever happens, David trusts God. He asks God to save him (1-7, 9, 11-12), to show him the way (8), and to sanctify him (10).

144 Happiness (144:3) □*□*□

As God's people we are a happy lot. We sing a new song. This Psalm relates to Psalm 18. In verses 5-7, David lists seven actions he wants God to make. God is David's source of victory (1-8) and his song of victory (9-15).

145 Praise God (145:2) □*□*□

David wrote this acrostic Psalm to praise his great God. But there are 21 verses, not 22 as the Hebrew alphabet would require. The "nun" letter is supplied in the Dead Sea Scrolls and comes between verses 13 and 14 and reads thus: "The Lord is faithful in all His words, and gracious in all His works." David praises God's greatness (1-6), His goodness (7-10), His glory (11-14) and His grace (14-21).

146 Hallelujah (146:5) □*□*□

We praise the Lord because he is special in many ways. God is eternal and dependable (1-4, 10). He makes us happy and is our Hope and Creator (5-6). He helps us in at least nine ways (6-9). The last five psalms all start and end with "Praise the Lord."

147 Reasons to Praise God (147:3) □✱□✱□

After the Babylonian captivity and exile, Jerusalem was restored. When the King of Kings returns, there will be a New Jerusalem. The Jews and we can praise God for at least four reasons: For God's work with Israel (2, 13-14, 19-20), for His work with nature (8-10, 15-16), for His work with the heavens (4-5) and for His work with the redeemed (3, 6, 11).

148 God's Glory (148:13) □✱□✱□

The universal choirs sing praises to God's glory. This choir is made up of all creation, of all animals, of all stones. The topmost section of the choir is made up of angels (1-6), then come the great sea creatures and trees (7-10), then all the kings and people (11-12), and in the front row the children of Israel (13-14). In front is the Lord who is being praised. "Praise the Lord" is here repeated 13 times.

149 Joyful Praise (149:2) □✱□✱□

Jesus is coming again. The saints sing praises to him with a new song of experience. They praise the Lord with their mouths and with music. They know the Lord and have walked with Him (1-6). They also reign with Him and bind the kings in judgment (6-9)

150 True Worship (150:2) □✱□✱□

The last of the psalms tells us where to worship, why worship and how to worship (1-5). At least seven types of musical instruments are in this orchestra (3-5). The word "praise" is used 13 times. This psalm reminds us that the psalms are not only prayers and poems, but also musical experiences. The praise of God is to be accompanied by musical instruments. As stated well in the Shorter Catechism, our purpose in life is to glorify God and to enjoy Him forever.

4 Praise him with the tumbrel and dance: praise him with stringed instruments and organs.

5 Praise him upon the loud cymbals: praise him upon the high sounding cymbals.

6 Let everything that hath breath praise the LORD. Praise the LORD.

.

About the Author

Rudy Klimes was born in Sternberk, Moravia, Czech Republic . He was a citizen of Czechoslovakia by birth, a citizen of Germany by proclamation, a citizen of Canada by naturalization. Since 1986, he is a citizen of the United States of America.

He lived under Hitler and Stalin and survived the holocaust and the Russian invasion. In 1948 he escaped from behind the iron curtain to live in Canada. Within three years, at the age of 19, he started teaching school, an occupation that has been his lifelong work.

He formally studied 11 languages and keeps a working knowledge of four of them, namely English, German, Korean and Japanese.

Rudy married Anna Homenchuk in 1954 and then attended Walla Walla College in Washington State. There he earned a Bachelor's and Master's degree in Education. Later he earned a Ph.D. from Indiana University, a Doctorate in Ministry from McCormick Theological Seminary, and a Master of Public Health from Johns Hopkins University.

Rudy and Anna worked as missionaries in the Far East for 26 years, first in Singapore, later in South Korea, Japan and Hong Kong. He served as president of colleges in the three countries that use chopsticks, namely Korea, Japan and Hong Kong. In 1969 Rudy received the Order of Civil Merit, the DongBaeg Medal, from the President of Korea.

Their three children, all born in Seoul, Korea, are Anita Heidi Borrowdale, MD, Bonnie Klimes-Dougan, PhD, and Randall David Klimes, BSEng. They have four grandchildren, Justin, Torin, Tyler and Hudson.

Upon returning from Japan, Rudy and Anna taught at Andrews University in Michigan, where Anna also received her Doctorate of Education. Later Rudy served as Associate Director of the Health and Temperance Department of the Adventist General Conference in Washington DC.

In 1994, Rudy and Anna returned to the USA and settled in Northern California. That year, they founded LearnWell Resources, a non-profit corporation that provides online continuing education and supports numerous charity projects, a number of them in the Ukraine.

Since 1995, Rudy has served also as associate pastor of a local church, making spiritual house calls and teaching the Bible. In that capacity, he also serves as a chaplain at Marshall Medical Center in Placerville.

Since 1997, Rudy teaches online health classes at Folsom Lake College as adjunct professor.

Praise God who has given Rudy these opportunities and have made him a pilgrim.

Appendix

1. Praying the Psalms by Athanasius of Alexandria

"In the *Psalter* you learn about yourself. You find depicted in it all the movements of your soul, all its changes, its ups and downs, its failures and recoveries."

My Dear Marcellinus,

I once talked with a certain studious old man, who had bestowed much labor on the *Psalter*, and discoursed to me about it with great persuasiveness and charm, expressing himself clearly too, and holding a copy of it in his hand the while he spoke. So I am going to write down for you the things he said.

Son, all the books of Scripture, both *Old Testament* and *New,* are inspired by God and useful for instruction, as the apostle says; but to those who really study it the *Psalter* yields especial treasure. Within it are represented and portrayed in all their great variety the movements of the human soul. It is like a picture, in which you see yourself portrayed and, seeing, may understand and consequently form yourself upon the pattern given.

In the *Psalter* you learn about yourself. You find depicted in it all the movements of your soul, all its changes, its ups and downs, its failures and recoveries. Moreover, whatever your particular need or trouble, from this same book you can select a form of words to fit it, so that you do not merely hear and then pass on, but learn the way to remedy your ill. Prohibitions of evildoing are plentiful in Scripture, but only the *Psalter* tells you how to obey these orders and refrain from sin.

"But the marvel with the Psalter is that...the reader takes all its words upon his lips as though they were his own, written for his special benefit..."

But the marvel with the *Psalter* is that, barring those prophecies about the Savior and some about the Gentiles, the reader takes all its words upon his lips as though they were his own, written for his special benefit, and takes them and recites them, not as though someone else were speaking or another person's feelings being described, but as himself speaking of himself, offering the words to God as his own heart's utterance, just as though he himself had made them up.

It is possible for us, therefore to find in the *Psalter* not only the reflection of our own soul's state, together with precept and example for all possible conditions, but also a fit form of words wherewith to please the Lord on each of life's occasions, words both of repentance and of thankfulness, so that we fall not into sin; for it is not for our actions only that we must give account before the *Judge,* but also for our every idle word.

"So, then, my son, let whoever reads this book of Psalms take the things in it quite simply as God-inspired."

When you would give thanks to God at your affliction's end, sing *Psalm 4*, *Psalm 75* and *Psalm 116*. When you see the wicked wanting to ensnare you and you wish your prayer to reach God's ears then wake up early and sing *Psalm 5*.

For victory over the enemy and the saving of created things, take not glory to yourself but, knowing that it is the Son of God who has thus brought things to a happy issue, say to Him *Psalm 9*; and when you see the boundless pride of man, and evil passing great, so that among men (so it seems) no holy thing remains, take refuge with the Lord and say *Psalm 12*. And if this state of things be long drawn out, be not faint-hearted, as though God had forgotten you, but call upon Him with *Psalm 27*.

If you want to know how *Moses* prayed, you have the *90th Psalm*. When you have been delivered from these enemies and oppressors, then sing *Psalm 18*; and when you marvel at the order of creation and God's good providence therein and at the holy precepts of the law, *Psalm 19* and *Psalm 24* will voice your prayer; while *Psalm 20* will give you words to comfort and to pray with others in distress.

When you yourself are fed and guided by the Lord and, seeing it, rejoice, the *23rd Psalm* awaits you. Do enemies surround you? Then lift up your heart to God and say *Psalm 25*, and you will surely see the sinners put to rout. And when you want the right way of approach to God in thankfulness, with spiritual understanding sing *Psalm 29*.

So, then, my son, let whoever reads this book of *Psalms* take the things in it quite simply as God-inspired. In every case the words you want are written down for you, and you can say them as your own.

2. Advice on Praying the Psalms, by Martin Luther

CONSIDER WHAT THE MOST respected church fathers, especially Athanasius and Augustine, taught about using psalms. They said we should adapt and adjust our minds so that we are in tune with the psalms. We must sing the psalms with the help of the Holy Spirit. They are like a school for the attitudes of the heart.

For example, when you read in Psalm 1, "Blessed is the person who does not follow the advice of wicked people," you must actually reject the advice that wicked people give you. When you read, "He delights in the teachings of the LORD," you shouldn't take it easy and pat yourself on the back as if you were a person who already loved the Lord's teachings. For as long as you live, you will need to think of yourself as a person who desperately needs to love God's teachings even more. When you read, "He succeeds in everything he does," you should wish this for yourself and feel sorry for those who find themselves in trouble.

Don't think that you are being asked to do the impossible. All you need to do is try, and I know you will be glad you did. First, practice on one psalm or even one verse of a psalm. You will be successful as soon as you have learned how to make just one verse come alive and live in your heart - even if it takes a day or a whole week. However, after you begin, everything else will follow naturally, and you will find a rich treasure of insight and love. Just be careful you don't let weariness and discouragement prevent you from getting started.

3. Connecting With God

"I stand at the door and knock. If anyone hears my voice and opens the door, I will come in to him and dine with him, and he with me."
Revelation 3:30

"I, God, stand at the door or your heart with an invitation to a banquet. If you hear my knocking and open the door of your inner being, I will come in to you and enjoy good food with you, and you with me. The Psalms are such spiritual feasts." (Author's paraphrase)

The Psalms are one of God's medium through which He shares Himself with our innermost self. With the Psalms, we can go beyond the printed word and into the spiritual kingdom of God. He stands at the door of our hearts and presents us with the Psalms as a wake-up call. He stands there and does not go away. He keeps knocking.

We have to listen to hear His knocking. If we do not hear the knocking, we cannot respond. We may think that there is nobody at the door of our hearts. We may think that there is no mindset of faith.

God invites us to respond. He has done His part. Now it is time for us to do our part. As long as the door to our heart is closed, we are fully in charge. We are protected from any invader.

God asks us to open the door of our heart and make ourselves vulnerable. He asks us to trust that when He comes in He will do us good and not harm. At the door of our houses, we usually open only to people we know and trust. We like to protect ourselves.

God comes in to stay and strengthen us. In the Psalms, He provides spiritual food. We enjoy it together, He and I. The conversation, while we eat, is heavenly. That is because the Psalms are for praying.

"The LORD's hand is not shortened, that it cannot save; neither his ear heavy, that it cannot hear: But your iniquities have separated between you and your God, and your sins have hid his face from you, that he will not hear." Isaiah 59:1-2.

It is not God who does not hear, but it is us who are not atune to His calling. We say prayers like we order sandwiches at a deli. There is a very big difference between saying prayers and really connecting with God and praying. The first is a recital of common words that express our desire, the second is an entering into God's spiritual kingdom and an uplifting of our souls to our Creator.

Our sins separate us from God. God still speaks and seeks us, but we cannot hear Him, and He cannot hear us. His words are lost on us, and our words are lost on Him. Sin is like a strong wall that stands between us and God.

When our sins make a barrier between us and God, then He cannot hear. Then there is not a live connection between us and God. Our main sin is selfishness. We get so concerned with our welfare and power that we forget the needs of others.

The Psalms are doors in the wall that give us access to God. When the Psalms are read, prayed, or sung with a receptive heart, God's voice gets through to us. When the Psalms are just a collection of poems, then the door is not open and we cannot hear God. The decision to open the door to our hearts is with us, not with God. He gives us that freedom of choice to open up or not to open up.

4. The Ten Commandments: Exodus 20:1-17

The Ten Commandments are easily made into prayers by adding "Lord, help me to..." in from of each one. They are not prayers in themselves, but answers to prayers for people who want to know what is the right and wrong way. They define the limits of the way of God. We are saved by trusting Jesus and accepting his gift of eternal life. As we follow Jesus, we walk in His way and try to avoid getting into trouble and sin. The list includes the first commandment (3), the second (4-6), third (7), forth (8-11), fifth (12) sixth (13), seventh (14), eights (15.), ninth (16) and tenth commandment (17).

1 And God spoke all these words, saying,

2 I am the LORD your God, which have brought you out of the land of Egypt, out of the house of bondage.

3 You shall have no other gods before me.

4 You shall not make unto yourself any graven image, or any likeness of anything that is in heaven above, or that is in the earth beneath, or that is in the water under the earth.

5 You shall not bow down yourself to them, nor serve them: for I the LORD your God am a jealous God, visiting the iniquity of the fathers upon the children unto the third and fourth generation of them that hate me;

6 And showing mercy unto thousands of them that love me, and keep my commandments.

7 You shall not take the name of the LORD your God in vain; for the LORD will not hold him guiltless that takes his name in vain.

8 Remember the Sabbath day, to keep it holy.

9 Six days shall you labor, and do all your work:

10 But the seventh day is the Sabbath of the LORD your God: in it you shall not do any work, thou, nor your son, nor your daughter, your manservant, nor your maidservant, nor your cattle, nor you stranger that is within your gates:

11 For in six days the LORD made heaven and earth, the sea, and all that in them is, and rested the seventh day: wherefore the LORD blessed the Sabbath day, and hallowed it.

12 Honor your father and your mother: that your days may be long upon the land which the LORD your God gives you.

13 You shall not kill.

14 You shall not commit adultery.

15 You shall not steal.

16 You shall not bear false witness against your neighbor.

17 You shall not covet your neighbor's house, you shall not covet your neighbor's wife, nor his manservant, nor his maidservant, nor his ox, nor his ass, nor any thing that is your neighbor's.

5. Bible Learning Activities

Start with a clear objective. Consider the time and resources available. Follow the individual interests and the skills of the participants. You may select one of the activities:

a. Art: murals, collage, paper tearing, cartooning, posters, montage, banners, bulletin boards, bumper sticker, badges, charts, graphs, painting, slides, stained glass picture.
b. Drama: puppets, role-play, pantomime, play, monologue, choral reading, dialogue, litany, psychodrama, skit, socio-drama.
c. Oral Communication: conversations, storytelling, interview, choral speaking, Bible reading, oral report, problem solving, workshop, book report.
d. Discussions: agree-disagree, circle responses, debate, in-basket, Question-Answer, word association, buzz groups, brainstorming, forum, panel discussion, case studies, symposium.
e. Creative Writing: letters, newspaper, poetry, short stories, diary, drama, acrostic, list, memo, outline, parable, paraphrase, prayers, self-evaluation, reaction sheets, group writing.
f. Music: singing, listening, writing songs, hymn study, jingle, guitar, sung paraphrase.
g. Research: books, records, video, Bible study teams, projects, surveys, display, exhibit, map study, collections, Bible games, time line.

Bibliography

Brueggemann Walter, Spirituality of the Psalms, Fortress Press, Minneapolis, 2002.

Klimes, Rudolf E., Joy Amid Stress, LearnWell Press, Folsom, 2005.

Klimes, Rudolf E., Trust Amid Trials. A Journey with James, LearnWell Press, Folsom, 2005

MacDonald, William, Believers Bible Commentary, Thomas Nelson Publishers, Nashville, TN, 1995.

Meyer, F. B., Choice Notes on the Psalms, Kregel Publications, Grand Rapids, MI, 1984.

Merrill, Nan C., Psalms for Praying, an Invitation to Wholeness, Continuum, New York, 2008.

The Bible, King James Version, Word Bible Publishers, Inc. 1611.

Weiser, Artur, The Psalms, Westminster John Knox Press, 2000

Wiersbe, Warren W., Be Exulted, Victor, Cook Communication Ministries, Colorado Springs, CO, 2004

Wiersbe, Warren W., Be Worshipful, Victor, Cook Communication Ministries, Colorado Springs, CO, 2004

Willington, Harold L., The Outline Bible, Tyndale House Publishers, Inc, Wheaton, IL 1999.

35315352R00078

Made in the USA
Lexington, KY
05 September 2014